Suzanne Lacasse, Education Services
National Gallery of Canada

Guide

D1430286

National Gallery of Canada
Ottawa, 1988

Canadian Cataloguing in Publication Data

National Gallery of Canada.
Guide.

Issued also in French under the same title.
ISBN 0-88884-579-0

1. National Gallery of Canada.
I. Lacasse, Suzanne. II. Title.

N910 07 A6 1988   708.11'384
                  C88-099505-X

Design: Tudhope Associates Inc.

Printed in Canada

Contents

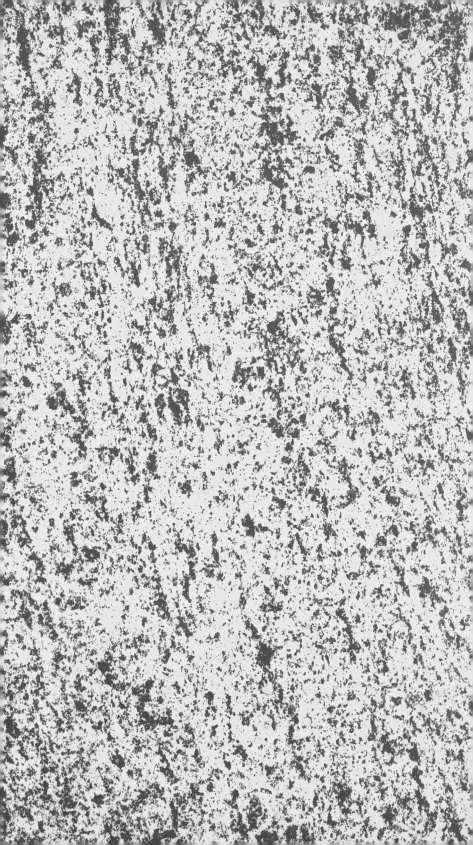

On 21 May 1988 a brand-new National Gallery of Canada opened its doors to the public, realizing at long last the dream of a permanent home. Today the collections and staff are under one roof, in quarters designed specifically for the collection, conservation, exhibition, and study of works of art.

Montreal architect Moshe Safdie, whose apartment complex Habitat (built for Expo 67) overturned conventional notions about city living, has created a magnificent structure. Airy, welcoming, and easily accessible, it has been described by Safdie as "a giant candelabrum in the heart of the community...everything about its design proclaims openness, the generosity of an act of invitation."

Landscape architect Cornelia Oberlander, whose work graces such major Canadian buildings as Arthur Erikson's courthouse in Vancouver, created the garden on the south side of the Gallery, which suggests the rugged northern terrain typical of the Group of Seven's paintings.

The galleries that house the collections are themselves superbly designed. Opening onto interior gardens and courts, they invite visitors to pause, to rest, to reflect, and above all, to enjoy the varied experiences offered by the Gallery. We hope that this *Guide* will help the visitor explore the Gallery and its rich and distinguished collections more easily.

The Canadian, European, and American collections are being fully documented in their respective catalogues, a continuing project of the curatorial and research staff. Copies of the first volumes in each series are available for interested readers in the Library and from the Bookstore.

Staff are always on hand to supply visitors with more detailed information; Gallery attendants, who can be identified by their tags, will refer questions to the appropriate person.

With justifiable pride in our new building, we extend an invitation to admire the spectacular architecture, to wander through the various exhibitions at leisure, and to make use of all the services provided for your comfort. A warm and sincere welcome!

Dr. Shirley L. Thomson, Director
National Gallery of Canada

Acknowledgements

The *Guide* was written in collaboration with the curators of the National Gallery of Canada: Charles Hill, Victoria Baker, Pierre Landry, and René Villeneuve (Canadian Art); Catherine Johnston, Michael Pantazzi, and David Ditner (European, American, and Asian Art); Diana Nemiroff and Susan Ditta (Contemporary Art); Rosemarie Tovell (Canadian Prints and Drawings); Marie Routledge (Inuit Art); Douglas Schoenherr (European and American Prints and Drawings); James Borcoman and Ann Thomas (Photographs).

For constant support and encouragement, I would like to thank my colleagues in Education Services, in particular, Michel V. Cheff, Barbara Dytnerska, Anne Newlands, Sylvie Tremblay, and Joanne Dagenais. Thanks are also due to Helen Clark, Susan Campbell, Charles Hupé, John Sargent, and Meva Hockley, who worked on assembling the photographs.

Finally, I would like to express my gratitude to the staff of the National Gallery's Publications Division: to Serge Thériault, Irene Lillico, and Micheline Ouellette, as well as to Marcia Rodriguez, English-language editor, and Jacques Pichette, French-language editor, sincere thanks.

S.L.

Canadian Galleries

On 6 March 1880, the Marquess of Lorne, then Governor General, inaugurated the first exhibition of the Royal Canadian Academy of Arts and at the same time announced the founding of the National Gallery of Canada. The diploma pieces submitted by the artists as a condition for membership in the Academy formed the nucleus of our national collection.

The nearly 800 paintings, sculptures, and decorative objects displayed in the large rooms devoted to Canadian art offer a survey of the history of art in this country. The arrangement respects both chronology — ranging from the religious sculpture and silver of eighteenth-century Quebec to the most avant-garde works of the 1960s — and regional characteristics, in order to do justice to the many facets of the Canadian creative spirit. The number of works exhibited as well as their undeniable quality ensure the uniqueness of the presentation.

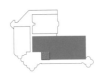

Most of the extant art from the period prior to the early nineteenth century is ecclesiastical. The Roman Catholic Church, aware of art's potential as a vehicle for religious instruction, commissioned works from architects, painters, sculptors, and silversmiths. Installed at the entrance to the Canadian galleries is the high altar of the old church at Longueuil. The tabernacle (fig. 1) was carved around 1741 by Paul Jourdain *dit* Labrosse; the altar table came from the studio of Louis Quévillon (1749-1823) around 1815. Two large paintings by Joseph Légaré (1795-1855), painted in 1821 for the church of Saint-Augustin de Desmaures in Portneuf, have been hung in the same gallery.

Other works on exhibition here are by artists such as Pierre-Noël Levasseur (1690-1770) and François Baillairgé (1759-1830), both from illustrious families of sculptors who were responsible for the ornamentation of many Quebec parish churches in the eighteenth and nineteenth centuries.

The decorative arts also flourished during this period, primarily because of the need for silver to be used in the liturgy. Among the most important silversmiths were Paul Lambert (1691 or 1703-1749), whose style was characterized by his use of the acanthus motif, and François Ranvoyzé (1739-1819). A selection of Ranvoyzé's work shows the development of his art up to the finest pieces, with their superb rendering of intricate plant motifs.

The Immaculate Conception by Salomon Marion (1782-1830), inspired by a French work now in the collection of Montreal's Musée de l'église Notre-Dame, is the only statue of its kind from this period and stands as a testimony to the virtuosity of Quebec silversmiths.

1. Paul Jourdain *dit* Labrosse
(1697-1769)

Tabernacle
c. 1741
Painted and gilt wood
172.2 x 280.8 x 65 cm

Canadian Galleries

Early Quebec Art
A101a

Early Quebec Art:
19th Century
A102, A102b

This gallery focuses on certain aspects of late eighteenth- and early nineteenth-century portraiture and domestic silver.

The great artists of the period include Jean-Baptiste Roy-Audy (1778-c. 1848), whose *Portrait of a Lady from Île Perrot* is exhibited here, François Beaucourt (see fig. 66), and William Berczy, whose celebrated *The Woolsey Family* was painted in 1809 (fig. 2). Considered his masterpiece, the painting demonstrates the skill and delicacy of execution that helped establish Berczy's reputation.

Stylistic correspondences exist between the silver and several of the paintings on display. For example, neoclassical influences similar to those in *The Woolsey Family* are evident in some of the works by Michael Arnoldi (1769-1807) and Robert Cruickshank (1773-1809).

The early nineteenth century witnessed considerable artistic diversification and increased production of secular works.

Although some artists crossed the Atlantic to complete their studies under European masters, usually in France, others, trained in Europe, immigrated to Canada.

Joseph Légaré, painter, politician, and ardent nationalist, was not only fascinated by the history of New France, but also depicted striking scenes of contemporary life such as *Cholera Plague, Quebec*, which in themselves are intriguing socio-political allegories.

Patronized by a flourishing bourgeoisie, Antoine Plamondon and Théophile Hamel (1817-1870) paved the way for profound changes in the art of portraiture, as seen in works such as Plamondon's *Soeur Saint-Alphonse* (fig. 3) and Hamel's *Portrait of Madame Lemoyne-Angers*.

2. William Berczy
(1744-1813)

The Woolsey Family
1809
Oil on canvas
59.8 x 87.2 cm
Gift of Major Edgar C. Woolsey,
1952

3. Antoine Plamondon
(1804-1895)

Soeur Saint-Alphonse
1841
Oil on canvas
90.6 x 72 cm

This new middle class desired not only portraits of themselves, but also paintings of their property, belongings, and even domestic animals, including horses and dogs. Robert Todd's two panoramic views of Wolfe's Cove, for example, were commissioned by the Gilmour family, owners of the shipyards portrayed (see fig. 4).

Illustrations of pastimes, including hunting scenes and other amusements, were also in great demand by the same middle class and by British soldiers stationed in the colony. This particular taste explains the success of Cornelius Krieghoff (1815-1872), who interpreted life and nature with an unparalleled enthusiasm not limited to any one genre. Paintings of sunsets, autumn landscapes, and winter scenes such as *Winter Landscape*, as well as representations of rural Canadian life such as *White Horse Inn by Moonlight* were all part of his repertoire.

The silver displayed in this gallery testifies to the skills and aesthetic concerns of several exceptional Quebec craftsmen, including Laurent Amiot (see fig. 5), Salomon Marion, and Pierre Huguet *dit* Latour (1749-1817). This last artist was responsible for renewing the art of ecclesiastical silversmithing, bringing to it the spirit of the Louis XVI style, at the same time using neoclassical elements in his domestic pieces.

4. Robert Clow Todd
(1809-1866)

*Wolfe's Cove, Quebec, at the
Heights of Abraham, Looking
East, Showing the Timber Yard
and the Sillery Shore*
1840
Oil on canvas
74.5 x 120.5 cm

5. Laurent Amiot
(1764-1839)

Monstrance
Silver (gilt) and glass
38.6 cm
Gift of Henry Birks & Sons Ltd.
1979

Canadian Galleries

Theme Room 1
A102a

The Rideau Street
Convent Chapel
A103

The Henry Birks Collection
of Canadian Silver

A102a   Room 1: The Patronage of the Arts in Early Canada

As a complement to the Canadian galleries and in an effort to help
visitors better understand the works displayed, four theme rooms
present a more thorough analysis of specific aspects of Canadian art.

A103   The chapel of the Convent of Our Lady of the Sacred Heart was
designed in 1887-88 by Canon Georges Bouillon and built on Rideau
Street in Ottawa (fig. 6). Noteworthy for the originality of its decorative elements, it features carved woodwork, cast-iron columns, arched
windows, and in particular, a neo-Gothic ceiling with wooden fan-vaults
painted grey, ochre, and blue.

The chapel, or more precisely, its decor and liturgical furnishings, were
recognized as having national architectural significance and saved from
the wrecker's ball in 1972. Dismantled and put into storage at that time,
it was finally reconstructed and restored inside the National Gallery.

In addition, this architectural treasure serves as a showcase for several
examples of religious statuary from the second half of the nineteenth
century, including the remarkable sculptures of Louis Jobin (1845-1928).
A variety of silver is also on display in this setting: consecrated vessels
and objects used in the liturgy are placed next to some of the presentation and commemorative pieces that were popular during the period.

Most of the ecclesiastical and domestic silver displayed in the galleries
comes from the Birks collection, which was begun in 1936 by Henry
Gifford Birks of Montreal and now comprises nearly 6,800 pieces. On
the occasion of the company's centennial in 1979, Henry Birks & Sons
Limited generously donated the collection to the National Gallery
of Canada.

6. Georges Bouillon
(1841-1932)

Interior Decor of the
Chapel of Our Lady of the
Sacred Heart Convent
(Rideau Street Convent)
1887-88
(Photograph, c. 1900)
Painted, varnished, and gilt
wood, cast iron, and glass
7.92 x 13.26 x 30.02 m

The nineteenth century saw the expansion of shipyards, military and civil administrations, and the forestry industry in the Maritimes; in Upper Canada, change came about through the growth of the agrarian economy, small industry, and the advent of the railways in the 1850s. It was this kind of socio-economic progress that supported artistic development.

The significance of Halifax for the Atlantic region is evident in the large painting *The Port of Halifax*, attributed to John Poad Drake (1794-1883). The city also attracted portraitists such as Robert Field (c. 1769-1819), who had already built an enviable reputation in the United States, and his successor William Valentine (1798-1849), both engaged by prominent citizens and the upper classes. John O'Brien's (1831-1891) paintings of ships, often depicted in stormy seas, are another testimony to the importance of maritime trade.

The history and development of Upper Canada (Ontario) could well serve as a backdrop to William Berczy's portrait of *Joseph Brant*, principal chief of the Six Nations. The painting presents Brant in the guise of a neoclassical hero and differs considerably from the portraits by Paul Kane, which have a unique historical value as documents of the life of the native Indians of western Canada at a time when the effects of colonization were already being felt (see fig. 69).

Robert Whale's views of Canada's flourishing cities, such as his *View of Hamilton*, also serve as valuable records of the special relationship that existed between the cities of the time and their natural environment.

Examples of silver works from the Maritimes complete the exhibits in this gallery.

Canadian Galleries

The Croscup Room
A104b

The Royal Canadian
Academy of Arts
A105, A105a

This set of murals painted on plaster once decorated the living room of shipowner William Croscup and his wife, Hannah, whose house was situated on Nova Scotia's north shore near Karsdale (fig. 7).

Painted around 1848 by an unknown artist, the murals (some of them inspired by engravings from the *Illustrated London News*) are an outstanding example of a form of decorative art that was popular along the Atlantic coast in the nineteenth century. The images, carefully arranged by the artist, include a family of Micmac Indians, views of Trafalgar Square and St. Petersburg, the launching of a ship, and overlooking the room, above the fireplace, Queen Victoria and her family receiving King Louis Philippe of France at Windsor Castle.

A105
A105a

Confederation in 1867 and the advent of the railways, which opened up territories previously accessible only with difficulty, helped to awaken a national consciousness. The picturesque, natural beauty of the new lands aroused the curiosity of Canadians, whose love of nature was unmistakable.

Although William Raphael (1833-1914) depicted immigrants arriving in Montreal, many artists clearly favoured more isolated locales.

7. The Painted Parlour of
Mr. and Mrs. William Croscup
c. 1846-48
Oil, charcoal, and graphite
on plaster
2.1 x 3.8 x 4.5 m

Lake Memphremagog, depicted by John A. Fraser (1838-1898) and Allan Edson (1846-1888), New Brunswick's Matapedia Valley, painted by Henry Sandham (1842-1910), and the countryside around the new summer resort areas near Tadoussac and the Malbaie, represented by Raphael and Lucius R. O'Brien, were all favourites with Canadian artists. O'Brien's *Sunrise on the Saguenay* is probably the most celebrated of these works (fig. 8).

The financial interests involved in the operation of the railways linking east and west also fostered development of the arts. Railway company directors, especially from the Canadian Pacific, bought works from artists, particularly those who had travelled across Canada and returned with pictures of the then unfamiliar Rockies.

Many of these artists were also among the founding members of the Royal Canadian Academy of Arts, created in 1880 by the Marquess of Lorne, Governor General at the time. Primarily landscape painters, they prepared the way for the emergence of a second generation of artists whose careers took shape in the 1880s and who completed their training in Paris. They produced a wide array of figurative art, following the European academic tradition, as evident in *A Venetian Bather* by Paul Peel (1860-1892), or in a more naturalistic vein, *A Wreath of Flowers* by William Brymner (1855-1925).

In both painting and sculpture, however, Canadian themes were predominant. Examples include *A Meeting of the School Trustees* by Robert Harris (fig. 9), *Mortgaging the Homestead* by George Reid

8. Lucius R. O'Brien
(1832-1899)

Sunrise on the Saguenay
1880
Oil on canvas
90 x 127 cm
Royal Canadian Academy
diploma work, deposited 1880

9. Robert Harris
(1849-1919)

*A Meeting of the
School Trustees*
1885
Oil on canvas
102.2 x 126.5 cm

Canadian Galleries

The Royal Canadian
Academy of Arts
A105, A105a

Late 19th Century
A106, A106a

(1878-1947), Louis-Philippe Hébert's (1850-1917) sculptures of contemporary political figures, and *Young Indians Hunting* by sculptor Alfred Laliberté (1878-1947), then at the beginning of his career.

The amassing of huge fortunes, the new cosmopolitanism of Montreal and Toronto, and the construction of large public buildings were among the main factors contributing to the emergence of a monumental style of painting at the turn of the century. All genres were affected, portraiture, in particular, becoming increasingly ostentatious. Artists such as William Blair Bruce painted large, decorative compositions in the style of the Paris salons, including *The Joy of the Nereids* (fig. 10). The allegorical approach also proved popular, as seen in *Hail Dominion!* by Gustav Hahn (1866-1962) and *Evening Harmony* by Marc-Aurèle de Foy Suzor-Coté (1869-1937).

This preoccupation with elegance and refinement was also reflected in sculpture, where similar allegorical themes were treated, as seen in *Inspiration* by Louis-Philippe Hébert and *The Storm* by Walter Allward (1876-1955).

The rediscovery of rural values by a young, urban society found expression in rustic themes. Although the subjects were realistically treated, the works were often tempered with a certain nostalgia, as seen in *De Profundis* by Horatio Walker (1858-1938).

The second gallery contains smaller works, paintings with more personal themes, and studies for large compositions, many by the same artists previously mentioned.

The focal point is undoubtedly the collection of paintings by Ozias Leduc, whose *The Young Reader* (fig. 11) presents an intimate view of his world.

Historical and nationalistic subjects remained popular, as demonstrated by sculptor Louis-Philippe Hébert's *The Last Indian* and the sketch *Dollard and His Companions* by Charles Huot (1855-1930).

10. William Blair Bruce
(1859-1906)

The Joy of the Nereids
1896
Oil on canvas
277.4 x 265.5 cm

A106b Room 2: Academic Training Abroad

A107
A107a
This gallery highlights various aspects of early twentieth-century Canadian painting and sculpture. The development and maturation of trends already hinted at in the 1890s can be seen in the symbolic landscapes of Ozias Leduc and the sculptures of Alfred Laliberté.

The period was characterized primarily by the integration of nationalist sentiments with international trends in art, and it was in this spirit that the Canadian Art Club was formed in 1907. The aim of the group, which existed until 1915, was to exhibit the works of Canada's best artists, whether they were living at home or abroad. In its drive to promote artistic excellence and ensure the advancement of Canadian art, the group sought the support of both collectors and the public.

The Canadian Art Club embraced artists working in different styles. Its founders included Edmund Morris (1871-1913), Curtis Williamson (1867-1944), and Homer Watson (1855-1936), who together with Horatio Walker favoured a sombre art inspired by Dutch painting and the work of the artists of the Barbizon school, who preferred landscapes and rural scenes.

Another tendency is represented by the winter scenes of Maurice Cullen (1866-1934) and Suzor-Coté, which reflect an impressionist fascination with vivid colours and light, an inclination also evident in the work of younger painters such as W.H. Clapp (1879-1954) and Clarence Gagnon (1881-1942).

A selection of paintings by James Wilson Morrice reveals the evolution of his work from turn-of-the-century Parisian views, through Canadian winter scenes and North African landscapes such as *Environs of Tangiers* (fig. 12), to depictions of the West Indies.

11. Ozias Leduc
(1864-1955)

The Young Reader
1894
Oil on canvas
36.7 x 46.7 cm

12. James Wilson Morrice
(1865-1924)

Environs of Tangiers
1912
Oil on canvas
65.5 x 81.7 cm

Canadian Galleries

The Canadian Art Club
A107, A107a

Water Court:
Sculpture 1900–1940
A116

Tom Thomson and the
Group of Seven
A108, A108a

The sculptors of the group include Phimister Proctor (1862-1950), who worked in the United States, and Walter Allward, represented here by plasters of an allegorical nature as well as by studies for public monuments.

Other aspects of Canadian nationalism are evident in such large-scale landscapes as Maurice Cullen's *Misty Afternoon, St. John's Newfoundland*, C.W. Jefferys's *Western Sunlight, Last Mountain Lake*, and Lawren Harris's *The Drive*, all illustrating a new appreciation of the immensity of the country.

A116   A selection of sculptures from the first half of the twentieth century occupies this courtyard. Statuettes and a bronze relief representing women factory workers from the First World War by Frances Loring (1887-1968) and Florence Wyle (1881-1968) of Toronto are exhibited along with *1914*, a work by Henri Hébert (1884-1950) that evokes the horrors of war.

A self-portrait by Alfred Laliberté shows us the artist who created *Head of a Woman* (fig. 13) and *Muse*, a beautiful, sensuous work in white marble.

The monumental *Eskimo Mother and Child*, a work carved in stone by Frances Loring, and *Torso* by Florence Wyle reflect the more naturalistic and classical tendencies of sculpture in the thirties.

A108   Around the same time as the Canadian Art Club was promoting an art
A108a based on national pride yet still European in perspective, a number of Toronto artists were developing a philosophy and style of painting that would find its inspiration and reason for being in the Canadian landscape. Working at Georgian Bay, in Algonquin Park, and later in the Algoma region, these artists were less inclined to produce a faithful reproduction of a "terre sauvage" than to express its ruggedness as a symbol of the country itself.

13. Alfred Laliberté
(1878-1953)

Head of a Woman
1923-28
Marble
44.7 x 24 x 24.5 cm

14. Tom Thomson
(1877-1917)

The Jack Pine
1916-17
Oil on canvas
127.9 x 139.8 cm

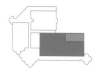

Canadian Galleries

Tom Thomson and the
Group of Seven
A108, A108a

Theme Room 3
A108b

The Group of Seven
A109

This gallery documents the period from 1913 to 1920 — the years of exploration that preceded the formation of the Group of Seven and the work of its future members. It also focuses on the tragically brief career of Tom Thomson, who was the group's inspiration.

Besides Thomson's celebrated painting *The Jack Pine* (fig. 14), the gallery contains equally well-known works such as *Terre Sauvage* and *Red Maple* by A.Y. Jackson (1892-1974), *The Guide's Home, Algonquin* by Arthur Lismer (1885-1969), *Snow (II)* by Lawren Harris (1885-1970), *The Tangled Garden* by J.E.H. MacDonald (1873-1932), and *Gipsy Head* by Fred Varley (1881-1969).

A number of oil sketches done from nature in vivid colours and free brushstrokes evoke the intensity of the artists' experience of the Canadian wilderness.

A108b Room 3: The Beginnings of Modern Art in Canada

A109 Although the First World War scattered the members of the group, they reunited in May 1920 to form the Group of Seven. The goal of these artists — Franklin Carmichael, Lawren Harris, A.Y. Jackson, Franz Johnston, Arthur Lismer, J.E.H. MacDonald, and Fred Varley — was to create a completely original art, which would in itself express the Canadian reality.

Two themes recur throughout their works. The first presents the tree (often a dead or windswept tree) as a symbol; examples include Lismer's *A September Gale, Georgian Bay*, Varley's *Stormy Weather, Georgian Bay*, and Harris's *North Shore, Lake Superior* (fig. 15). The latter painting, together with MacDonald's *The Solemn Land*, demonstrates the spiritual impact of Canada's vast northern landscapes. This second theme captured the imagination of these artists who sought to define the essence of Canada, and led them far beyond the boundaries of northern Ontario to the Rockies and even to the Arctic.

15. Lawren S. Harris
(1885-1970)

*North Shore,
Lake Superior*
1926
Oil on canvas
102.2 x 128.3 cm

16. J.E.H. MacDonald
(1873-1932)

The Supply Boat
1915-16
Oil on beaverboard
121.2 x 238.2 cm
Gift of
Mr. and Mrs. H.R. Jackman,
1967

Canadian Galleries

The MacCallum–
Jackman Cottage
A109a

Montreal: 1920–1940
A109b

The Canadian Group
of Painters
A110

The panels painted by Tom Thomson, J.E.H. MacDonald, and Arthur Lismer for the cottage of their patron, Dr. James MacCallum, are unique in the history of Canadian mural painting. Commissioned by Dr. MacCallum in 1915, these panels evoke the history of Georgian Bay, its inhabitants and plant life, and the flavour of summer life of the time (see fig. 16).

Mr. and Mrs. Harry Jackman of Toronto donated these works to the Gallery in 1969, in emulation of the generous spirit of Dr. MacCallum, who had bequeathed 134 paintings (including 83 by Tom Thomson) to the Gallery in 1943.

A109b   Although landscape was the dominant subject of Canadian painting in the 1920s, in Montreal the artists were primarily concerned with figurative painting.

For the most part products of Parisian schools, these artists, who united briefly under the banner of the Beaver Hall Hill Group, adhered to both academic and contemporary traditions. Born of an urban, cosmopolitan background, their work was characterized by an exploration of the plastic and formal qualities of painting.

Despite Edwin Holgate's *Ludivine* (fig. 17) being one of the best-known works produced by these painters, and although Adrien Hébert's (1890-1967) harbour scenes have also drawn attention, the majority of these artists were women. They included, among others, Prudence Heward (1896-1947), who painted *Girl on a Hill*, and Lilias Torrance Newton (1896-1980), whose *Self-portrait* is part of the collection.

A110   After J.E.H. MacDonald's death in December 1932, the Group of Seven decided to broaden its membership and formed the Canadian Group of Painters in an effort to unite artists across Canada and to support individual expression.

17. Edwin Holgate
(1892-1977)

Ludivine
c. 1930
Oil on canvas
76.3 x 63.9 cm
Vincent Massey Bequest,
1968

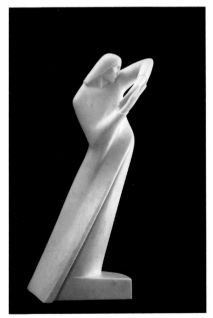

18. Elizabeth Wyn Wood
(1903-1966)

Gesture
c. 1930
Saravezza marble
99.5 x 45.5 x 44 cm

Canadian Galleries

The Canadian Group
of Painters
A110

British Columbia:
1900–1950
A110a

The group initially showed a preference for landscapes. However, like many artists, Carl Schaefer's treatment of the genre in *Ontario Farm House* transformed landscape into an expression of his geographical and social roots, situated in the context of the thirties.

Others, following the trail blazed by Lawren Harris, sought a modern approach suited to their own generation, based on clean lines and pure forms. The sculptures of Elizabeth Wyn Wood (see fig. 18) and the abstractions of Bertram Brooker were attempts to express a reality that transcended time.

Yet other artists, such as New Brunswick's Jack Humphrey and Miller Brittain and Montreal's Sam Borenstein, found a harsh source of inspiration in the immediate reality of the Great Depression. The authenticity with which they depicted their urban environment served as an important reference point for the artists who documented the experience of Canadian soldiers during the Second World War.

Also represented here are works by Quebec artist Marc-Aurèle Fortin (1888-1970), who shows certain similarities to his contemporaries in his choice of the city and the port as subjects. However, it is clear from *Landscape Ahuntsic* that his work is distinguished by a quality that is both plastic and decorative at the same time.

A110a Emily Carr is undeniably British Columbia's foremost painter of the first half of the twentieth century. This gallery offers a survey of her works, from the early paintings done in France and the Indian villages of the West Coast to *Blunden Harbour* (fig. 19), a monumental and mystical composition. The artist's mature works, oil paintings on paper, consist of landscapes, which become more and more luminous and airy in their great swirls of colour.

19. Emily Carr
(1871-1945)

Blunden Harbour
c. 1930
Oil on canvas
129.8 x 93.6 cm

20. David Milne
(1882-1953)

Trees in Spring
1916
Oil on canvas
55.8 x 66.1 cm
Gift of Douglas M. Duncan,
1968

Canadian Galleries

British Columbia: 1900–1950
A110a

David Milne and
L.L. FitzGerald
A110b

The Contemporary Arts
Society and Alfred Pellan
A111

Fred Varley, one of the Group of Seven who had come from Toronto in 1926, exerted a strong influence on artistic activity in Vancouver. His was a spiritual art imbued with Oriental philosophy, interpreting landscape and the symbolic role of colour. Varley's *Vera*, painted in subtle shades of green, and Jock Macdonald's (1897-1960) enigmatic landscape *Pilgrimage* are representative of these directions.

In the forties and fifties, E.J. Hughes (b. 1913) depicted the life and landscape of the West Coast in vibrant colours and a naive spirit, while B.C. Binning (1909-1976) turned these subjects into elegant, formal abstractions, tinged with whimsy.

A110b Working first in the United States and later in isolated regions of Ontario, David Milne pursued an original approach based on visual perception (see fig. 20). In treating the canvas as a surface composed of lines and colours, he explored the relationships between man and nature. He painted simple objects with restraint and left only the "explosive substance" to act on the sensibility of the viewer.

Winnipeg's L.L. FitzGerald painted with equal restraint. He limited himself to drawings and small canvases depicting his environment, where with small, skilfully juxtaposed strokes, he constructed an architectonic world bathed in a diffuse light.

A111 In founding the Contemporary Arts Society in 1939, John Lyman (1886-1967) united almost all of Montreal's progressive artists in the common pursuit of a living art.

Inspired by early twentieth-century French painting, these artists used an expressive style to interpret a variety of subjects: landscapes, still-lifes, portraits, nudes, and street scenes.

21. Alfred Pellan
(b. 1906)

On the Beach
1945
Oil on canvas
207.7 x 167.6 cm

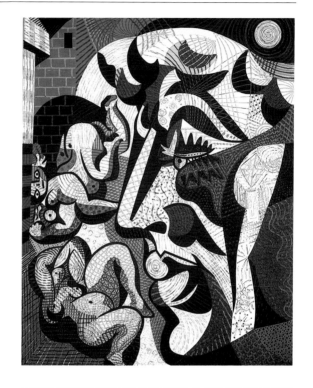

22. Paul-Émile Borduas
(1905-1960)

Leeward of the Island
1947
Oil on canvas
114.7 x 147.7 cm

Canadian Galleries

The Contemporary Arts
Society and Alfred Pellan
A111

Early Automatistes
A111a

Automatistes and Plasticiens
A112

This bent towards European painting was further stimulated by the return to Montreal of Alfred Pellan in 1940, who, although a native of Quebec, had lived in Paris since 1927. He brought back a surrealistic and figurative painting, sometimes inspired by literature, in which he juxtaposed forms and objects in an imaginative world of dreams and nightmares (see fig. 21). Pellan's influence is evident not only in the paintings of younger artists but also in the sculpture of the period.

A111a   The pictorial explorations of Paul-Émile Borduas led him from representational painting to abstract art. Inspired by Surrealism and Freudian theories, he expressed his inner self through automatic writing, and together with his students created a world of explosive, symbolic forms rendered by vigorous strokes and dark, saturated colours (see fig. 22).

This liberation of the subconscious gave the Automatistes an awareness of the necessity of social freedom, which became the central theme of their 1948 manifesto, *Refus Global*.

A112   After moving to the United States in 1953 and to Paris two years later, Borduas painted increasingly airy, subtle works, finally realizing large, spatial compositions rendered in black and white.

Jean-Paul Riopelle first as Borduas's student and after 1946 when he was working in Paris, investigated the expressive qualities of colour, creating enormous, dense, structured compositions in tones as vibrant as medieval stained-glass windows or autumn leaves (see fig. 23).

Other Montreal artists rejected the premises of Automatiste painting, which was based on the release of the subconscious, and instead formulated a theory that considered an object as autonomous and dissociated from its sources. Composed of geometric forms and limited tones, their works suggest a new relationship between intention and intuition. These artists, known as the Plasticiens, offer us a world in which the energetic qualities of colour become a structural element.

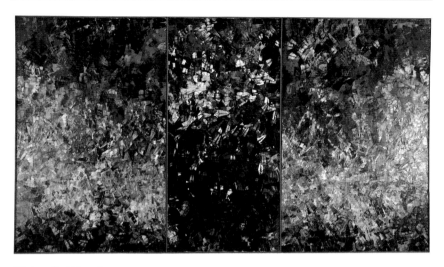

23. Jean-Paul Riopelle
(b. 1923)

Pavane
1954
Oil on canvas
300 x 550.2 cm

24. Alex Colville
(b. 1920)

Couple on Beach
1957
Casein tempera on masonite
73.4 x 91.4 cm

Canadian Galleries

Theme Room 4
A112a

Realist Traditions
A112b

The 1950s and 1960s
A113–A114a

A112a   Room 4: Abstract Painters in Their Own Words

A112b   Post-war painting offered Canadian artists a variety of paths, which
included abstract (either linear or expressive), representational, or
figurative art. A number of artists, schooled by the socio-realist movements of the thirties, displayed great originality in their interpretation
of those movements' concepts.

Quebec's Jean-Paul Lemieux (b. 1904), obsessed by the passage of
time, expresses the solitude in which we live. In an austere style
designed to achieve greater simplicity, he portrays his figures in front
of vast empty spaces, creating an atmosphere of melancholy and reverie.

Maritime painter Alex Colville depicts figures frozen in action, in
compositions that haunt the viewer with the intensity of the moment
and the prospect of imminence (see fig. 24).

In Toronto, William Kurelek (1927-1977) drew on his childhood
memories of Ukrainian prairie life to create works at once descriptive
and moralistic.

A113 –   Abstract or non-representational painting dominated Canadian art in
A114a   the 1950s and took on many different forms, depending on the artist
and on regional trends. As in the work of Montreal artists, one can
define a superficial polarity between expressive, gestural painting and
a more geometric, analytical style. The former can, as in the work of
Vancouver's Jack Shadbolt (see fig. 25) express a lyrical and subjective
interpretation of nature, or in the work of Toronto's William Ronald
(see fig. 26) an aggressive and subjective dynamism. The latter ranges
from the vibrating gongs of Claude Tousignant (see fig. 27) to the
iconic images of Regina's Art Mackay and Ronald Bloore. Nature
remained a vital source for some artists, as is evident in the flowing,
interlocking forms of Jock Macdonald's later works. But for others, the
city and its new technology became the stimulus, as witnessed by the
television parts incorporated into Harold Town's collage *Music Behind*.

25. Jack Shadbolt
(b. 1909)

Winter Theme No. 7
1961
Oil and lucite on canvas
108 x 129.2 cm

26. William Ronald
(b. 1926)

The Hero
1957
Oil on canvas
183 x 183 cm

Artists during the fifties still felt the need to define themselves collectively, to make a stance for contemporary art, as did Painters Eleven in Toronto and to a certain degree the Regina Five. With the increasing public acceptance of contemporary art in the sixties, this need to band together around an ideology yielded to the formation of groups of artists, such as Vancouver's Intermedia, wishing to share creative and technological resources.

Ideas initiated in the fifties saw fruition in the great variety of scale, shapes, and languages of the works produced in the sixties. New attitudes developed towards figuration, subject matter, technology, the contemporary environment, and even to the art object itself. The boundaries that had traditionally separated the various media were no longer adequate: three-dimensional objects could be incorporated into painting or film narration used as a device in assemblages. The ideas were what mattered, and to express those ideas any means were valid.

To do justice to the multiplicity of artistic expression, and to the many artists active during the period, temporary exhibits will be set up in these rooms. The displays will consist of selections of paintings and sculptures focusing on specific regions, movements, and affinities.

27. Claude Tousignant
(b. 1932)

Gong 88, No. 1
1966
Acrylic on canvas
223.5 cm (diameter)

European and American Galleries

A few years after it was founded in 1880, the National Gallery lay the foundation of a collection of European art, which was enriched over the years owing to the efforts of a succession of directors, curators, and chairmen of the Board of Trustees.

By the early 1950s, the collection already numbered some four hundred works, including important paintings by Piero di Cosimo, Cranach, Bronzino, Veronese, El Greco, Poussin, van Dyck, Murillo, Rigaud, Canaletto, Turner, Courbet, Degas, and van Gogh. Between 1953 and 1956, the museum had the opportunity to acquire a dozen major works from the Prince of Liechtenstein, among them pictures by Filippino Lippi, Rubens, Rembrandt, and Chardin. Beginning in 1966, another series of major acquisitions was undertaken, substantially enlarging the collection of nineteenth- and twentieth-century art. During the same period, the museum also purchased a number of sculptures, including splendid examples of Bernini, Puget, and Clodion, as well as a painting by Baldung, which became the focal point of the small but very fine group of German works.

During the 1970s, works by Lotto and Poussin were added, then in succession, works from the seventeenth and eighteenth centuries by Annibale Carracci and Philippe de Champaigne, a youthful composition by Jean Restout, and, later, a panel painting by van Orley. A number of works of decorative art were also acquired, adding a new dimension to the collection.

The collection is located on the second level and the works are presented in chronological order, beginning with the Middle Ages and leading up to the 1960s and the American avant-garde.

The works exhibited in this gallery are evidence of a vital period in
the visual arts in Italy. The majority are on religious themes, including several panels that once formed part of multi-panelled altarpieces
painted in tempera on a gold background.

Stylistically, these earlier paintings derive from one of the two major
central Italian workshops: that of Duccio in Siena and Giotto in
Florence. Simone Martini trained in Duccio's workshop and his *St.
Catherine of Alexandria* (fig. 28), originally part of an altar at Orvieto,
is marked by the elegant, linear style of Sienese painting. Jacopo di
Cione's *Triptych of the Virgin and Child Enthroned with Saints*
(c. 1370-80) is a Florentine work from the second half of the fourteenth
century in which Giotto's more robust influence dominates. Remarkably
well preserved, it is a portable tryptich for personal devotion. Well
over fifty years later at the height of the Florentine Renaissance,
painters would attach great importance to the volumetric rendition of
figures and the representation of space by means of perspective, as
seen in such works as Neri di Bici's *Assumption of the Virgin* (1455-56)
and Benozzo Gozzoli's *Virgin and Child with Saints* (1476-77?).

Filippino Lippi's *Triumph of Mordecai* and *Esther at the Palace
Gate* (c. 1475-80) are two small, extremely fine panels on the theme
of marital fidelity, which were part of a series of six decorating two
cassoni or chests that contained a bride's dowry.

Piero di Cosimo's *Vulcan and Aeolus* (1485-90), with its mythological
subject set in a landscape, is representative of the Renaissance interest
in classical learning (the basis of modern humanism), an interest that
focused in particular on man and his mastery of the world around
him. The picture is the earliest example of a painting on canvas in
the collection.

28. Simone Martini
(c. 1284-1344)

St. Catherine of Alexandria
early 1320s
Tempera on wood
82.2 x 44.5 cm

29. French (Romanesque)
Relief: Lion (fragment)
1100-1299
Limestone
39.6 x 29.9 cm

European and
American Galleries

Italy: 14th and 15th Centuries
C201

France: Medieval Sculpture
C201a

Northern Europe:
15th and 16th Centuries
C202, C202a

Among the sculptures in this gallery are *Nude Warriors with Horses* (late fifteenth century), two terracotta reliefs that were formerly part of a decorative frieze on the Fodri palace in Cremona. The use of terracotta is typical of northern Italy; in Florence, marble was the popular medium. *The Virgin and Child* (c. 1485) is among the finest reliefs attributed to the Master of the Marble Madonnas, and is unusual for having retained most of its original colours.

C201a This group of works, consisting primarily of decorative capitals from French churches and monasteries of the twelfth century, was acquired in 1972. Stylistically, they display all the richness and originality that resulted from the convergence of diverse cultural currents. Among the most popular motifs were the fanciful animals (see fig. 29) inspired by manuscript illuminations, textiles from the Near East, and decorative elements derived from classical antiquity. In medieval Western Europe, capitals were among the preferred means of religious instruction. Drawing inspiration from the reliefs on Roman sarcophagi, sculptors illustrated episodes from the Old and New Testaments in simple forms that convey the subject in a direct and lively manner.

C202
C202a A work of private devotion from Cologne, *The Madonna of the Flowering Pea* (c. 1425) is remarkable for its great sensitivity and elegance of design. Memling's *Virgin and Child with St. Anthony Abbot and a Donor* (fig. 30) reveals the new realism typical of Flanders, which liberated religious painting from its conventions: the subject is depicted in a contemporary domestic setting with a landscape in the background. In *The Crucifixion* (c. 1520), by Quentin Matsys, the emphasis on landscape is more pronounced. The scene, represented in a traditional manner in the foreground, is set against a vast, extremely detailed landscape in which Jerusalem takes on the appearance of a Flemish walled town. This use of landscape contributing to a new definition of space in religious art remained common in painting throughout Northern Europe until the sixteenth century.

The trend toward realism would lead to more intimist scenes, such as Bernard van Orley's *The Virgin and Child* (c. 1518-20). This devotional panel, particularly noteworthy for its refinement and attention to detail, was part of a diptych commissioned by Margaret of Austria, regent and governor of the Netherlands until 1530. The other half of the diptych, now lost, represented her kneeling in adoration before the holy pair.

The inclusion of the donor in many religious works, adorned in his or her finest attire, and the increasing popularity of portrait painting evidence the importance of an emerging social class (made up in part of rich merchants) that gave rise to a new humanism. At the same time, the development of new techniques in painting using oils and glazes allowed artists to create subtle effects suggesting the materiality of flesh, precious objects, and fabrics.

Portrait of a Bavarian Prince (c. 1531) by Barthel Beham is one of the most remarkable portraits in the collection. Painted according to the Italian mode of half-length portraits, it conveys the subject's personality and suggests the texture of the fabrics with great effect. Also from Germany are the marriage portraits (c. 1544) of Christian von Conersheim and his wife, Elisabeth von Brauweiler, by Barthel Bruyn the Elder. The paintings are in their original arched black and gold frames, typical of the era.

In the later fifteenth century, Northern Europe began to experience a spiritual upheaval that culminated in Luther's Protestant Reformation in 1517. Artists such as Hans Baldung made use of moralistic themes from the Bible, as in *Eve, the Serpent, and Death* (c. 1510-1515), a macabre depiction of the fall of Man. In contrast, a major work by Lucas Cranach the Elder, a *Venus* (c. 1518) inspired by mythology and Italian painting, is a pretext for the portrayal of a sensual female nude. Probably painted for the Saxon court, the work is signed with a winged serpent, the artist's trademark.

European and
American Galleries

Northern Europe:
15th and 16th Centuries
C202, C202a

Italy: 16th Century
C203

Exhibited along with the paintings are two German examples of poly-chrome wood sculpture: an anonymous *Virgin and Child on the Crescent Moon* (c. 1500) from Franconia (late fifteenth—early sixteenth century), and *The Magdalen* (c. 1520) from the circle of Jörg Lederer.

C203 During the period from the early Renaissance to the sixteenth century, a number of Italian cities became flourishing artistic centres. Renaissance humanism reached its zenith in Florence and Venice and at the courts of Ferrara, Mantua, Urbino, and Milan.

Dosso Dossi's *Aeneas at the Entrance to the Elysian Fields* (1521) was painted for the court of Alfonso d'Este in Ferrara. The work was part of a frieze composed of ten scenes from the *Aeneid*; its literary-mythological subject and depiction of landscape bear witness to the new spirit of the Renaissance. *The Christ Child and the Infant John the Baptist with a Lamb* by the Milanese Bernardino Luini is reminiscent of Leonardo da Vinci, from whom Luini borrowed the subtle modelling of light and shade and the manifest interest in the precise depiction of plants.

In *The Virgin and Child with SS. Roch and Sebastian* (1521-24) by Lorenzo Lotto (who worked primarily in Bergamo and the Veneto), the figures of the saints express strong emotions. The exaggerated contortions of the bodies, accentuated by the contrast of unusual colours, are characteristic of the new style of the period called Mannerism, a courtly style that would reach an exceptionally high degree of sophistication and elegance.

Bronzino's *Portrait of a Man* (fig. 31) is a typically Mannerist work, particularly in the aloof expression of the aristocratic sitter and the exaggerated elongation of his fingers. The sculpture placed in the background is a witness to the subject's cultivated taste.

30. Hans Memling
(c. 1433-1494)

The Virgin and Child with
St. Anthony Abbot and a Donor
1472
Oil on wood, cradled
92.7 x 53.6 cm

31. Bronzino
(1503-1572)

Portrait of a Man
early 1550s
Oil on wood, cradled
106.7 x 82.5 cm

European and
American Galleries

Italy: 16th Century
C203

17th Century
C204, C205a

Around 1475, the Renaissance was felt in Venice and the arts flourished anew, leading to masters such as Titian and the generation of Veronese and Tintoretto, whose work would dominate the sixteenth century. Veronese's *The Repentant Magdalen* (c. 1560-75), with its diagonal composition and dramatic expression of emotions in fact anticipates Baroque painting.

C204
C205a
The works in this gallery are primarily from those countries where the Catholic Church, in an attempt to counteract the Reformation, experienced a renewal that deeply affected religious art and architecture.

Sculpture attained a rare level of excellence with the work of Gian Lorenzo Bernini, friend and protégé of Pope Urban VIII (Maffeo Barberini). Bernini executed several portraits of his patron, one of which — a marble bust — is part of the collection (fig. 32). Despite the nature of the material and the official character of the work, the sculptor interpreted with great sensitivity the sitter's expression, heightened by the precise rendering of the beard and the wrinkles around the eyes.

By the dramatic use of diagonals and a complex compositional structure, Nicolas Poussin demonstrated his mastery of the Baroque style in *The Martyrdom of St. Erasmus* (1628). This *modello* is a preliminary oil sketch for one of the high altars in the nave of Saint Peter's in Rome, one of the most celebrated paintings of the period. The frame, a later addition, is nevertheless contemporary with the sketch and is decorated with the bee and the laurel, the emblems of the Barberini family, who commissioned the work. In Salvator Rosa's moving *The Return of the Prodigal Son*, the influence of Caravaggio can be discerned in the contrast of shadow and light and in the realistic depiction of the figures.

Seville's fame as an important artistic centre in seventeenth-century Spain was due in part to the reputation of one of its sons, Bartolomé Esteban Murillo. The largest work by Murillo in the collection is *Abraham and the Three Angels*, originally part of the magnificent decorations of the Hospital de la Caridad in Seville.

32. Gian Lorenzo Bernini
(1598-1680)

*Maffeo Barberini,
Pope Urban VIII*
c. 1632
Marble
94.7 x 68.8 x 34.3 cm
(with base)

33. Jacob Jordaens
(1593-1678)

*As the Old Sing,
So the Young Pipe*
early 1640s
Oil on canvas
145.5 x 218 cm

European and
American Galleries

17th Century
C204, C205a

Northern Europe:
17th Century
C205

Another great centre of European Baroque art was the Flemish city Antwerp, then under Spanish occupation, where both Rubens and van Dyck worked in the service of the Catholic Church and the regents of the Hapsburgs.

Though primarily a portrait painter, van Dyck also painted religious and mythological subjects. In his *Suffer Little Children to Come Unto Me* (c. 1618), an early work, he interpreted a biblical theme in a contemporary context; it has been suggested that the figures to the right may be the painter Rubens and his family.

Jacob Jordaens, a student of Rubens, produced along with mythological and religious scenes, highly original allegorical and genre scenes. Among these, *As the Old Sing, So the Young Pipe* (fig. 33) takes its subject from a Flemish proverb, which Jordaens was to reinterpret several times. This boisterous banquet, at which the artist has represented the members of his family, portrays, in fact, both his anti-Spanish political opinions and his moral values, as the various symbolic elements incorporated into the picture indicate.

A number of French artists lived for a time in Italy, studying and working at the very sources of classical antiquity. Among these were the sculptor Pierre Puget, whose *Bust of a King* (c. 1667-68) is in the collection; the painter Simon Vouet, who as a student was greatly influenced by Caravaggio, as is evident in his *The Fortune-teller* (c. 1620); and Claude Lorrain, who painted *Landscape with a Temple of Bacchus* (1644). It was in Italy that Claude developed a concept of ideal landscape painting, famous for subtle atmospheric effects and imaginary settings inspired by classical architecture.

Remarkable for virtuosity of execution is a work attributed to Lorenzo Vaccaro, *St. George and the Dragon* (c. 1695), one of the few surviving examples of domestic Neapolitan sculpture in silver. The head and limbs of Saint George and the maiden, as well as the cherubim at the base, are cast in silver, while the other elements are of gilded bronze.

Dutch landscape painting is represented by the masters and disciples of two distinct schools. Jan Both, trained in Rome, adopted Claude Lorrain's radiant effects of light, which he transposed to rustic scenes such as his *Landscape with Hunters* (c. 1650). Hobbema, however, followed the lead of his master, Jacob Ruisdael, and remained more faithful to the reality of the Dutch countryside. In *Two Water-mills*, he achieves effects of depth by opposing to the shadow in the foreground the light areas of the background.

Portraits held an important place in a society in which social rank counted at least as much as personality. *Portrait of a Seated Man* (c. 1645) by the great Dutch portraitist Frans Hals is an unusually informal work in which the sitter appears to address himself directly to the viewer. In contrast, Peter Lely's elegant and formal *Sir Edward Massey* (c. 1647) shows the extent to which van Dyck's formulas influenced and dominated official portraiture.

Emmanuel de Witte's *A Sermon in the Old Church at Delft* (c. 1650-51) is one of the earliest works of a new genre, the depiction of church interiors. De Witte's style is characterized by a special interest in architectural form, oblique views, and the play of light and shadow. The same preoccupation with light and its effects is evident in *The Lacemaker* (1655) by Nicolaes Maes, which movingly captures the individual absorbed in her work.

The admirable realism, indeed the extreme attention to detail in Jan Davidsz de Heem's *Still-life with Fruit and Butterflies* (c. 1645-55?) reflects the taste for riches of the new bourgeoisie. Yet the work is at the same time an allegory of all that is beautiful but transitory in this world.

European and
American Galleries

Northern Europe:
17th Century
C205

Theme Room
C206

Venice:
18th-Century Painting
C207

A few Flemish works are also on view in this gallery. Among them, Rubens's *The Entombment* (c. 1612-14), which may have been intended as a devotional work, is a variation on an altarpiece by Caravaggio that Rubens saw during a stay in Italy. Rubens, however, infused it with his personal style, changed some of the figures, and tightened up the composition. The work comes from the collection of the princes of Liechtenstein, whose seal it still bears.

Now considered the greatest of Dutch painters, Rembrandt's work was also highly prized during his lifetime. *Heroine from the Old Testament* (fig. 34), which represents either Esther or Bathsheba, reveals his dramatic use of light to stress the brilliance of flesh and the sumptuous quality of the costumes. Jan Lievens, who in his youth shared a studio with Rembrandt, rivalled Rembrandt's ingenuity in his use of chiaroscuro and depiction of character, as is evident in his *Job* of 1631.

C206   This gallery will be used for the temporary display of works on paper or for didactic exhibitions complementing the works in the adjoining galleries.

C207   Venice was in the forefront of artistic innovation during the eighteenth century, and it was here that a new genre, the *veduta* or view painting, was largely developed. During this period, Italy was host to many travellers, who, wishing a record of the sights they admired, directly stimulated the birth of this new genre. Venice's incomparable splendour made it a popular choice among amateurs of *vedute*.

34. Rembrandt van Rijn
(1606-1669)

Heroine from the Old Testament
1632-33
Oil on linen
109.2 x 94.4 cm

35. Canaletto
(1697-1768)

*St. Mark's and the
Clock Tower, Venice*
1735-37
Oil on canvas
132.8 x 165.1 cm

European and
American Galleries

Venice:
18th-Century Painting
C207

Great Britain: 18th Century
C208

Long a favourite of English art patrons, Canaletto was the best known of Venetian view painters. His earlier and finest work is highly original in its sense of composition and dramatic handling of light, qualities exemplified in *St. Mark's and the Clock Tower, Venice* (fig. 35). The picture was part of a series commissioned by the Englishman William Holbech for his country house, Farnborough Hall. Bernardo Bellotto, who was both Canaletto's nephew and apprentice, achieved an equal degree of fame as a view painter. His *The Arsenal, Venice* (c. 1743) shows the entrance to the famous dockyard in which were built the ships of the powerful Venetian navy that had long dominated the Mediterranean.

The works of Francesco Guardi, such as *The Church of S. Maria della Salute, Venice* (early 1780s), show a preference for a vibrant and poetic treatment of light and colour. The artist sacrifices detail for overall effect and suggests the essential with a few deft brushstrokes.

French painter Claude-Joseph Vernet, who spent many years working in Rome, produced scenes such as *View of Lake Nemi* (1748). The work is characterized by a meticulous attention to light as well as a keen and sensitive observation of nature. A related spirit also informs an urban landscape by Dutch painter Isaak Ouwater, entitled *The Westerkerk, Amsterdam* (1778).

C208 During the Georgian era, economic prosperity and a new influx of ideas from the Continent led to an artistic renewal that culminated in the establishment in 1768 of the Royal Academy. Nevertheless, a traditional British interest in portrait and landscape painting remained high, and the Academy's first president, Sir Joshua Reynolds, was a famous portraitist. His *Colonel Charles Churchill* (c. 1755) portrays the son-in-law of Sir Robert Walpole, the British prime minister. A few years before, Gawen Hamilton painted *Thomas Wentworth, Earl of Strafford, and His Family* (1732), an early example of the conversation piece, a (usually) small-scale group portrait in which the sitters are engaged in conversation or other social activity.

The work of Thomas Gainsborough is represented by the interesting oval portrait (1768) of Ignatius Sancho, a former slave who achieved considerable fame as a poet and art critic, and the more sombre portrait of *The Reverend William Stevens* (c. 1780).

Some of the paintings in this gallery portray events from Canada's history. There is, for instance, *Joseph Brant (Thayendanegea)* (c. 1776) by George Romney, painted when Brant, a Mohawk chief, was in London to discuss with George III's government the involvement of his own tribe and of other Six Nations tribes in the American Revolution. Dressed in his native costume, he is wearing a silver gorget given to him by the British king. Joshua Reynolds executed a portrait of *Sir Jeffrey Amherst* (1768) after Amherst's return to England as governor of British North America, following the capture of Louisbourg (1758). The posthumous bust of *General James Wolfe* (c. 1760) portrays him as a classical hero, notwithstanding the gorget he is wearing, which is similar to Joseph Brant's. In contrast, Benjamin West's *The Death of General Wolfe* (fig. 36) represents him in contemporary terms, and includes portraits of a number of persons who served with Wolfe, although they were not actually present at his death. This painting, the first version exhibited at the Royal Academy in 1771, was followed by several other versions. West, an American, became George III's official painter and succeeded Joshua Reynolds as President of the Academy.

Richard Wilson's *A Distant View of Rome from Monte Mario* (c. 1763-65) reflects the English taste for classical landscape, evident in the numerous works by Poussin and Claude in British art collections of the period. The burlesque scene in Philip James de Loutherbourg's *A Midsummer's Afternoon with a Methodist Preacher* (1777), however, betrays a knowledge of the satiric and moralistic works of William Hogarth. In George Morland's *Wreckers* (c. 1790), the turbulent sky and the grim subject (thieves deliberately run ships onto the rocks in order to steal the cargo) introduce the notion of the sublime — that is, the terrifying aspects of nature and man — greatly admired towards the end of the eighteenth century.

The works assembled in this gallery, principally portraits, reveal diverse achievements in Italy and Spain as well as the distinct evolution of portrait painting from its rather formal, earlier mode to the later, more intimate and familiar genre.

The portraits of Spanish painter Francisco Bayeu have often been confused with those of his brother-in-law, Goya. Despite the dignified pose and elegant costume, Bayeu's *Portrait of a Man* (c. 1785-90) is more candid in its depiction of the sitter than is commonly expected from formal portraiture.

Italian artist Giuseppe Baldrighi portrayed himself in the company of fellow-painters in *The Artist and Two Friends* (c. 1751-56). This original composition, showing an animated conversation among the three friends, freezes an instant in time. Just as obviously, it shows Baldrighi's interest in rendering specific facial expressions, derived from the *tête d'expression*, an academic exercise he had studied in Paris.

Pietro Rotari, an Italian painter who chose his models from the courts at Dresden and St. Petersburg, presents a fanciful portrait in *Young Woman with a Fan* (c. 1754-56). Well-known for this type of portrait, the artist gives the work an intimate character.

Also on view is a carved group, *Guardian Angel*, once part of the decorations of the Ursuline Convent in Vienna. It is a fairly unusual example of Austrian art, in that the application of silver leaf, such as on the angel's flowery robes, is generally more characteristic of Spanish and Portuguese Baroque sculpture.

36. Benjamin West
(1738-1820)

The Death of General Wolfe
1770
Oil on canvas
153.7 x 213.4 cm
Presented by the
Duke of Westminster to the
Canadian War Memorials,
1918

37. Jean Siméon Chardin
(1699-1779)

The Return from the Market
1738
Oil on canvas
46.7 x 37.5 cm

European and
American Galleries

Continental Europe:
18th Century
C208c

Neoclassicism
C209

The eighteenth century was a particularly flourishing period for the arts in France. Under the aegis of the Academy, founded in 1648, the hierarchy of genres was fundamental and any artist who wished to succeed was forced to conform to it to some extent.

Until the mid-nineteenth century, history painting, which included religious and mythological subjects, was considered the most elevated genre. Jean Restout's *Venus Presenting Arms to Aeneas* (1717) falls within this category and was, in fact, painted as a diploma piece for his admission to the Academy. The dynamic composition faithfully renders a passage from the *Aeneid*. Restout places the accent on the hero, and depicts his reaction to the prophecy of the fall of Rome.

Second in rank in the eyes of the Academy was portrait painting. In *Jean Le Juge and His Family* (1699), court painter Hyacinthe Rigaud produced a work still Baroque in spirit, in which the sumptuous setting emphasizes social rank at the expense of the psychology of the sitters.

Jean Siméon Chardin was responsible for revitalizing and popularizing genre painting in France. His work is splendidly represented by *The Return from the Market* (fig. 37) and *The Governess* (1739), both of which depict ordinary people attending to their daily tasks. A master of still-life painting, Chardin was equally adept at conferring an almost magical presence on everyday objects and conveying the warmth and poetry of domestic life.

C209   Towards the end of the eighteenth century, art reflected a renewed interest in antiquity and classical Rome, an interest that was closely associated with the philosophical and social changes sweeping Europe at the time. Beginning around 1780, painting was characterized by a simplified composition, linear forms, and a sober treatment of the subject.

38. Antonio Canova
(1757-1822)

Dancer
c. 1818-22
Marble
172.7 cm

European and
American Galleries

Neoclassicism
C209

Great Britain and France:
19th Century
C211

The study of classical sculpture permeated virtually every genre of painting, and is evident in works as diverse as the *Portrait of Madame Begon de Misery* (1807) by Girodet, *Bacchus and Ariadne* (c. 1821), a history painting by Gros, and particularly in *The Shepherd Paris* (c. 1785), a nude study attributed to Jean-Germain Drouis.

Joseph Chinard, the most successful French sculptor of the Consulate and the Empire, endowed his bust of *The Empress Josephine* (1805) with her fabled beauty. Interestingly, her somewhat melancholy expression appears slightly at odds with the ornate jewellery and the extraordinary dress decorated with Napoleonic emblems.

The greatest sculptor of the neoclassical period was Antonio Canova. His *Dancer* (fig. 38) is the second version of a celebrated work he executed for the Empress Josephine. The work displays all the delicate grace to which Neoclassicism aspired, combining, as it does, the ancient with the modern and the natural with the ideal.

Two objects of decorative art from this period evoke the ancient works that inspired them. This inspiration is evident in Benjamin Smith's and Digby Scott's two-handled cup and cover (1805), whose form is derived from the krater, a red clay vase found in ancient Greece. The fascination with and reverence for antiquity is also obvious in a sardonyx bowl, which is actually a Roman object from the first century A.D. transformed into a lamp around 1810 by the addition of a Medusa head and a figure of Psyche in gilded bronze.

Inspired by eighteenth-century theories on the sublime and the beautiful, English artists of this period adopted a more sensitive and individualized approach to nature. In France, artists rejected the rigorous style and treatment of neoclassical painting and chose subjects of a more expressive nature from history or literature, rendering them in a highly personal, passionate style. A painting such as Eugène Delacroix's *Othello and Desdemona* (c. 1847) reflects the Romantic era's taste for dramatic incidents involving love and death. The painting illustrates the scene in which Othello, convinced that Desdemona has been unfaithful, enters her chamber intent on strangling her.

Camille Corot's *The Bridge at Narni* (1827), an early work, still belongs to the French tradition of composed landscape, ultimately derived from Claude and Poussin. Through careful observation of a specific site, the artist produced a calm, serene, and intelligible view of nature, which he placed in an ordered but vibrant composition.

In order to describe nature as faithfully as possible, John Constable depicted subjects he knew well and had observed repeatedly, such as *Salisbury Cathedral from the Bishop's Grounds* (c. 1820). He thus achieved a vision of the world animated by a spiritual force that orders and organizes nature.

J.M.W. Turner's typically awe-inspiring vision of nature may be seen in his *Mercury and Argus* (fig. 39), a work much admired by John Ruskin in *Modern Painters*, published in 1843. Although the painting retains elements of traditional idealized landscape, such as a luminous sunset, these elements are combined with the sense of the spectacular unique to the artist, so that the work attains a truly Romantic theatricality.

Painted during a visit to Egypt, Jean-Léon Gérôme's *Camels at the Watering-place* (1857) is one of the first paintings to reflect the contemporary interest in Orientalism.

The excesses and lyricism of Romanticism provoked a reaction that was directly inspired by nature, rural life, and contemporary society. This movement, known as Realism, attempted to give an objective view of the world.

In the forefront of the Realist movement, painter Gustave Courbet achieved considerable fame despite adverse official reaction to his work. In the series of landscapes painted in Étretat, including *The Cliffs at Etretat* (1866), he revealed the majesty of nature bathed in light, using thick layers of paint to better convey the solidity of the rock.

Although Honoré Daumier is remembered primarily for his caricatures, he also produced intensely moving portrayals of everyday life. As an innovator in this genre, he depicted such modern scenes as waiting rooms and omnibuses. In *The Third-Class Carriage* (1863-65), the impact of the subject is heightened by the enclosed space where sombre tones express the tragedy of the human condition.

Jean-François Millet portrayed peasant life while infusing it with a spirit of nobility. He shows the peasant hunched over his work or attending to the tasks of farm life, as in *The Pig Slaughter* (1867-70).

39. J.M.W. Turner
(1775-1851)

Mercury and Argus
c. 1836
Oil on canvas
151.8 x 111.8 cm

Dissatisfied with the art instruction prescribed by the Royal Academy in England, younger artists, among them Dante Gabriel Rossetti and William Holman Hunt, developed an interest in the simple forms of Italian painting that preceded Raphael and the High Renaissance. In *The Salutation of Beatrice* (fig. 40), Rossetti reveals his attachment to the medieval, pre-Raphaelite world by taking his inspiration from the work of Dante and by idealizing the spiritual and physical beauty of woman, incarnated in Beatrice.

Frederic Leighton's work represents the persistence of the academic tradition in late nineteenth-century England. Although he was also interested in medieval and Biblical subjects, Leighton, a future president of the Royal Academy, stressed the classical aspect of his nudes with pure, linear contours in works such as *Actaea, Nymph of the Shore* (1868).

American James McNeill Whistler broke with the tradition of British painting as practised in the 1860s and 1870s. In *Lillie in Our Alley* (c. 1898), the effect of the refined tones and the mood of the work exceed the more literal requirements of portrait painting, but are consistent with his attraction to "art for art's sake."

Walter Richard Sickert's *The Old Bedford: Cupid in the Gallery* (c. 1890) reveals how much he was influenced by French painting, particularly by Edgar Degas, an artist whom he greatly admired and with whom he shared a taste for concert halls. Sickert also painted genre scenes and landscapes, generally using a low-key, chromatic scale with dark, warm tones.

40. Dante Gabriel Rossetti
(1828-1882)

The Salutation of Beatrice
1859
Oil on panel
101 x 202 cm

41. Camille Pissarro
(1830-1903)

The Stone Bridge in Rouen,
Dull Weather
1896
Oil on canvas
66.1 x 91.5 cm

The works assembled in this gallery represent Impressionism, its influence, and subsequent reactions to it (see also room C215). The Impressionists were primarily concerned with spontaneously recording their perception of nature. Painting out of doors, then a revolutionary concept, they attempted to capture the fleeting aspect and colour of the world around them as it was constantly modified by light. Preoccupied with the mechanism of vision and opposed to any form of official art, the Impressionists favoured landscapes and cityscapes.

In retrospect, Claude Monet was the exemplary Impressionist painter. His *Waterloo Bridge: The Sun through the Fog* (1903) is an eloquent proof. The contours are blurred by brushstrokes, and the soft, misty colours add to the hazy atmosphere, with a single lively colour accenting the play of sunlight and its reflection on the shimmering water.

In Camille Pissarro's *Hay Harvest at Eragny* (1901) the brilliant, primary colours are painted with short, broken brushstrokes. True to the Impressionist point of view, the contours of forms dissolve gradually to disappear in the glare of the light. *The Stone Bridge in Rouen, Dull Weather* (fig. 41) shows Pissarro's particular interest in urban landscape, once again unveiled in the brilliant daylight.

Edgar Degas was interested in the world that peopled the opera-stage, the singers and clients of the café-concerts, or simply the everyday world that surrounded him. *Woman with an Umbrella* (c. 1876), a work he left partly unfinished, reveals him as a powerfully realist painter who unambiguously records his sitter's intense, haughty gaze and chilly reticence.

Paul Cézanne's brushwork and clear colours show the degree to which he sympathized with Impressionism. Nevertheless, like Degas, he was interested in expressing the more permanent aspects of nature, its underlying form and structure. In later works such as *Forest* (1902-04), the assertion of form is somewhat less pronounced, and his work appears more closely aligned with that of some of his Impressionist friends.

Soon after the first Impressionist exhibitions, artists began to develop different modes of expression. Van Gogh, among others, evolved an expressive style, as is evident in *Iris* (1889), in which forms are forcefully underlined and the vivid colours are applied with a vigorous brushstroke.

Jackson Pollock was one of the first artists to adopt "action painting"
by letting the paint flow, drip, or squirt over the entire canvas. His
No. 29 (fig. 42) was uncharacteristically painted on glass to allow a
movie camera to record the artist at work from the other side of the glass
pane. This new movement, better known under the generic term
Abstract Expressionism, marked the beginning of the New York School,
and became the basis of subsequent artistic trends in the United States.

Developing, for the most part, a highly individualistic style, some
artists such as Barnett Newman (see fig. 46) reacted against the
emphatic outlook of Abstract Expressionism and moved toward chromatic abstraction, according considerable importance to the simplified
expression of colour. Others such as Milton Resnick chose a more
intimate style, characterized by an interest in the physicality of paint.
In *Saturn* (1976), Resnick applied layer upon layer of matter to create
an impressively thick, heavily textured crust.

The same reaction to extreme forms of expression and gestural
improvisation can be observed in the sculpture of the period. Tony
Smith's *Black Box* (1962-67) is an example of a new trend in sculpture of the 1960s, characterized by a high degree of simplification, the
adoption of geometric forms, and the use of industrial materials, in

42. Jackson Pollock
(1912-1956)

No. 29
1950
Oil, expanded steel, string,
glass, and pebbles on glass
121.9 x 182.9 cm

European and
American Galleries

The United States after 1945
C214

Early 20th Century
C215

this case, steel. The work is thus liberated from the constraints of representation and can attain an independent status with its own, separate existence, distinct from the necessity of giving the illusion of something else. The viewer shares the space of Donald Judd's works such as *Untitled* (1974), in which the simple but commanding repetitious forms generate a sense of order.

C215   The linear, decorative qualities of the work of Viennese artist Gustav Klimt link it to the Art Nouveau style that was popular at the turn of the century. His *Hope I* (fig. 43) nevertheless reveals the profoundly symbolic and visionary aspect of his painting, in which he expresses the struggle between life and death and his confidence in the continuity of life.

In James Ensor's *Skeletons in the Studio* (1900), the Belgian artist's luminous palette of bright colours serves as a vehicle for his strange and fantastic subjects. In this very personal work, the artist satirizes his critics, whom he reduces to skeletons.

Dutch artist Kees van Dongen's *Souvenir of the Russian Opera Season* (1909) evokes the sensual languor of dance through the use of brilliant colours and the stylized curves of the dancers' bodies. The picture commemorates an important event in the history of modern dance and music: the famous 1908 season that Diaghilev's Ballets Russes spent in Paris.

Nude on a Yellow Sofa (1926) by Henri Matisse affirms his predilection for the female nude, vigorously modelled and placed in a decorative setting. In sculptures such as *Large Head* (1927), the artist shows himself just as absorbed by the study of form, here raised to an even higher degree of geometric purity.

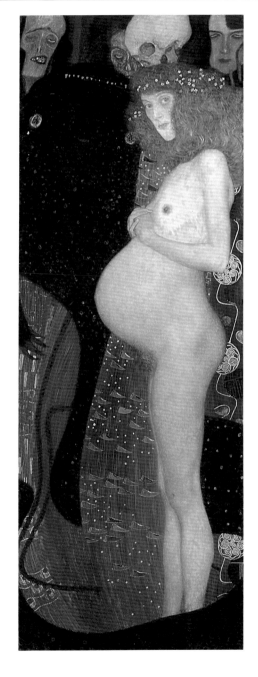

43. Gustav Klimt
(1862-1918)

Hope I
1903
Oil on canvas
189.2 x 67 cm

Until the first decades of the century, British painting remained fairly conservative. However, under the influence of Impressionism and later, Futurism, movements in art began to reflect interests in parallel with developments on the Continent.

William Orpen's portraits of women display a great simplicity, the light falling on their faces in contrast with the more sombre tones of their clothes. John Lavery's *Grey Owl* (1935) is a portrait of the writer who under this pseudonym became a successful chronicler of life in the Canadian forest. Wilson Steer's landscapes reveal an Impressionist preoccupation with light, without adopting the fragmented treatment.

The National Gallery is indebted to the Massey Foundation, which, between 1946 and 1950, donated eighty-eight paintings collected by the Right Honourable Vincent Massey between 1935 and 1946, while he was the Canadian High Commissioner to Great Britain. The collection includes the main figures in British art from the generation of 1900 to about 1946.

C216a Augustus John was probably the most important British portrait painter in the first half of the twentieth century. At first his interest was in landscape, which he treated in a post-impressionist manner, at the same time preserving an element of primordial simplicity. A prolific portraitist, he stripped his subjects of all artifice, representing them in a direct, sober fashion, as is evident in *Lawrence of Arabia* (1935) and *Canadian Soldiers* (c. 1917).

44. Francis Bacon
(b. 1909)

Study for Portrait No. 1
1956
Oil on canvas
197.7 x 142.3 cm

European and
American Galleries

Great Britain: 20th Century
C216a

International Modernism
C216

Henry Moore re-established British sculpture on an even footing with painting, after it had been long relegated to second place. Moore experimented with problems of form, which he opened up and hollowed out in an attempt to find a visual equilibrium between matter and void. The human body, particularly the female body, remained for him a constant, favourite theme. *Reclining Woman* (1930), one of his early works, is a study in volume and evokes the primitive character of the Mexican sculpture that inspired it.

Francis Bacon's work startles by its disquieting, shocking vision of the human condition. In *Study for Portrait No. 1* (fig. 44), he suggests the isolation of man trapped within his internal world of suffering with the horrid depiction of a silent scream, the almost imperceptible lines of a cage, and the violent colour of the robes, evocative of danger and cruelty.

C216   After 1900, artists began to be concerned with formal questions in which means of expression became the principal vehicle for artistic theory. They were interested, for example, in the relationship between the flat surface of the canvas and the illusion of three-dimensional form, or yet again, by the relationship between the external appearance and the internal logic of a subject's construction. Yet psychology, contemporary political life, and the economic reality of the time all played equally important roles.

Picasso's concern with form is particularly apparent in *The Small Table* (1919), a Cubist still-life. The artist emphasized the contours of various objects, fragmented their forms, then reassembled them in a harmonious composition on a single plane, thus eliminating the illusion of depth.

Jacob Epstein's *Rock Drill* (1913-16), like Fernand Léger's *The Mechanic* (fig. 45), integrates human and mechanical forms in order to express the alienation of modern man in an industrial world. Both artists use a formal vocabulary in which geometry and representation overlap.

45. Fernand Léger
(1881-1955)

The Mechanic
1920
Oil on canvas
116 x 88.8 cm

European and
American Galleries

International Modernism
C216

Marcel Duchamp
C217

Dutch artist Piet Mondrian chose to exclude any reference to the natural world in order to explore, without reference to a subject, the formal values of line, colour, and surface. In *Composition 1936-1942*, the importance accorded to order and equilibrium is stressed by the calculated positioning of pure colours.

Surrealism, as interpreted by artists such as Salvador Dali and inspired by modern psychology, focused primarily on exploring the subconscious through the interpretation of dreams and by using free-association. Dali explained that *Gala and the Angelus of Millet...* (1933) was the result of a vision he had of Millet's painting *The Angelus*, which prompted him to create a number of works freely associating elements of that work with other images.

In the years following the Second World War, American artists began to see non-figurative painting as the most spontaneous and immediate way of expressing the creative energy of the subconscious.

C217   In 1913, French artist Marcel Duchamp defined all traditional aesthetic concepts and produced the first of a series of works that he called "ready-mades," which were wholly or partly composed of randomly found industrial objects. The ready-made was then replicated as a challenge to the concept that a work of art is unique (fig. 47).

46. Barnett Newman
(1905-1970)

The Way I
1951
Oil on canvas
101.6 x 76.2 cm

47. Marcel Duchamp
(1887-1968)

Bicycle Wheel
1913-64
Bicycle fork with wheel
mounted upside-down on
painted wooden stool
126 x 64 x 31.5 cm

Asian Galleries

The National Gallery acquired its first Asian work of art in 1913. Now numbering almost four hundred remarkably diverse works, the collection spans a period from the third century A.D. to the modern era. This collection was made possible in large part by the generosity of a number of benefactors, in particular Max Tanenbaum, who, starting in 1978, donated the impressive group of works of Indian art, once part of the collection of Nasli and Alice Heeramaneck of New York.

The works in this gallery represent the major periods and regional schools of Indian art.

The first two groups of sculptures show in succession works from the Kushan and Gupta periods (A.D. 100-500), which witnessed the foundation of the great classical styles of Indian art. The next group contains works from the Pala dynasty, which illustrate Buddhist iconography (see fig. 48).

The works from the medieval period (A.D. 600-1200), the second great period of Indian art, adhere to the stylistic canons derived from the Gupta period but show a distinct taste for more complex compositions and greater animation (see fig. 49). In the late medieval period, sculpture flourished, particularly in the Hoyshala dynasty in the south of India and the Pratihara dynasty in the north.

Also on view are examples of bronze sculpture; large numbers of these were produced in Kashmir, Nepal, Tibet, and southern India beginning in the tenth century. Representing both Hindu and Buddhist subjects, these works cover a wide range of styles from the simple to the richly complex.

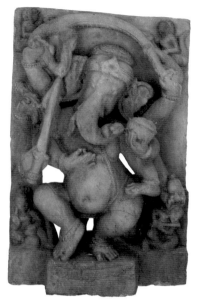

48. Indian (Bihar)
Buddha Shakyamuni
Pala period, 10th C.
Sandstone
71.2 cm
Gift of Max Tanenbaum, 1978

49. Indian
Ganesha Dancing
10th C.
Sandstone
58.4 cm
Gift of Max Tanenbaum, 1978

Contemporary Art

The period spanned by the contemporary collection — from the early 1960s to the present — has been characterized by an active questioning of both the material limits and the theoretical basis of art. An important result of contemporary artists' inquiries into what art can be has been an explosion of traditional categories. In addition to painting and sculpture, the contemporary collection includes films, sound recordings, videos, multi-media installations, and a wide variety of works on paper, from prints and drawings to posters and photographs. Even the necessity that a work of art be an object at all has been questioned: certain works in the collection are purely written statements of an idea.

The emphasis of the collection is on Canadian art. Since Eric Brown's directorship in the years of the Group of Seven, the National Gallery has championed the work of the most innovative living Canadian artists and has built a substantial collection of their work. At the same time it has recognized regional diversities, and represents the work of promising younger artists alongside that of the more established.

The Gallery began collecting American art in the late 1960s, in response to the vitality and growing importance of the New York art scene at the time. More recently, works by European, South American, and Japanese artists have been acquired, allowing the work of contemporary Canadian artists to be considered in a truly international context.

At present the collection of contemporary art is one of the largest in the country, comprising some 1,500 works, including more than 300 videos by artists and an important collection of installation works. With galleries on two levels and a two-storey courtyard providing over 3,000 square metres of exhibition space, the range of the collection can now be represented more fully than ever before. The galleries on the lower level focus on the years between 1960 and 1980, and feature the work of Canadian and foreign artists arranged according to the movements or concerns they represent. The upper-level galleries are reserved for changing installations of work from 1975 to the present, which highlight recent directions in contemporary art and bring new acquisitions to the attention of the visitor.

By the 1960s modernism was firmly entrenched in Montreal and Toronto, continuing to find its primary expression in abstract painting and sculpture. Montreal artists Guido Molinari and Claude Tousignant were both making hard-edged geometric paintings of extreme simplicity, carrying the abstraction of the Plasticiens a step further. Unlike the earlier generation of vanguard artists, however, Molinari and Tousignant looked to New York rather than Paris, situating their own reassessment of pictorial space in a line of development that ran from Malevich and Mondrian to Pollock, Newman, Rothko, and beyond. Works such as Tousignant's *Chromatic Accelerator* (1967) or Molinari's *Orange and Green Bi-Serial* (1967) create a pictorial space based on the dynamic juxtaposition of contrasting bands of colour, rather than on an illusionistic figure/ground relationship.

Two independent figures in the Montreal art world, Yves Gaucher and Charles Gagnon were both strongly marked by their experience of contemporary American colour-field and abstract expressionist painting. Gaucher's *Grey on Grey* canvases (1967-69), in which a luminous field of colour is punctuated at random by fine lines of subtly contrasting greys, also reflect his early interest in the serial music of such composers as Anton Webern. Photographer and filmmaker as well as painter, Gagnon brings to his art an acute awareness of the eye's selective role and an interest in those things — a window, a doorway, a screen — that frame our experience of space. His *Cassation/Open/ Ouvert* (fig. 50) offers a framed space within a framed space, where the ambiguity between the two fields draws the viewer into a meditative relationship similar to that of Gaucher's *T-PB-11 J-JN-69* (1969).

The period of the 1970s in Toronto, as elsewhere in Canada, was one of intense experimentation that looked to similar developments in New York. The earlier predominance of painting gave way to sculpture, photography, sound, and mechanized elements in various combinations as artists explored the boundaries between art and everyday experience.

Typical of the multi-disciplinary artist who refuses to define himself in relation to any one medium is Michael Snow. Known internationally for his experimental films, Snow began his career as a painter and has since made extensive use of photography as a vehicle for his ideas. Framing as a metaphor for thought and perception links all of his work, providing unexpectedly witty results in his self-portrait *Authorization* (fig. 51), a work concerned with the process of its own making.

50. Charles Gagnon
(b. 1934)

Cassation/Open/Ouvert
1976
Oil on canvas
203.2 x 330.2 cm

51. Michael Snow
(b. 1929)

Authorization
1969
B/w photographs and cloth
tape on mirror in metal frame
54.6 x 44.4 cm

An equally versatile artist, Joyce Wieland is also an unequivocal femi-
nist and Canadian nationalist. Her quilted assemblages, often made of
unconventional materials, give value to such traditionally feminine
occupations as needlework. At the same time, works such as *Reason
over Passion* (fig. 52), which memorializes the words of former Prime
Minister Pierre Elliott Trudeau, reflect an acute consciousness of the
inherent contradictions of politics.

Younger than Wieland and Snow, Ian Carr-Harris developed his work
in the pluralistic context of the seventies. He attempts to establish a
relationship between the reality of the work and that of the viewer by
using familiar objects for quite unexpected ends. Using texts, projected
images, or sound recordings, he creates provocative situations that
lead us to question our perception of reality and the expectations that
shape those perceptions.

Canada's geographical vastness has spawned a variety of regional
pockets of artistic activity. Some, like Montreal or Toronto, were
supported by the art market and a network of commercial and public
galleries; others, like London, were relatively isolated, but enlivened
by strongly independent artistic personalities.

52. Joyce Wieland
(b. 1931)

Reason over Passion
1968
Quilted cotton
256.5 x 302.3 cm

A firm sense of regional identity together with a resistance to imported cultural values forms the basis of London artist Greg Curnoe's art. His inspiration comes from his immediate environment, such as the view from his studio window of the hospital where he was born. As the dates in the title suggest, *View of Victoria Hospital, Second Series (February 10, 1969 - March 10, 1971)* (fig. 53) is a chronicle of passing time as well as a picture of a motif; together, the images, sounds, and words that make up the work reconstruct a passage in Curnoe's life.

An abiding interest in machines and an inventive mind of considerable originality have provided Murray Favro with the subjects and means of much of his sculpture. From flying machines like his scaled-down version of a sabre jet to environmental reconstructions of two-dimensional images such as *Synthetic Lake* (1973) or *Country Road* (1971-72), his work is based on applying the principles of observation and experimentation to the understanding of his own experience.

Paterson Ewen came to London in 1968 after having already established himself as an abstract painter in Montreal. His attraction to meteorology and astronomy inspired a series of semi-abstract paintings of natural phenomena, which culminated in such masterful landscapes as *Moon over Tobermory* (fig. 54).

53. Greg Curnoe
(b. 1936)

*View of Victoria Hospital,
Second Series*
1969-71
Oil, wallpaper, stamp-pad ink,
graphite, plexiglas, metal,
loudspeakers, magnetic sound
tape and tape recorder,
electrical wire, and eight-page
printed text on plywood
243.8 x 487 cm

54. Paterson Ewen
(b. 1925)

Moon over Tobermory
1981
Acrylic and metal on
gouged plywood
243.8 x 335.9 cm

Although abstraction began to lose ground as the predominant expression of modernism in the seventies, a number of artists have continued to make important contributions to this genre, including painter Ron Martin and sculptors David and Royden Rabinowitch.

Bright Red No. 8 (fig. 55) belongs to one of several series of single-colour paintings that Martin made in the early years of the decade, leading up to the all-black paintings that he worked on until 1981. Related in size to the human body, his works explore the materiality of paint while simultaneously offering themselves as analogies for human experience. The appearance of the paintings changes constantly depending on the vantage-point from which they are seen, as does the appearance of the Rabinowitch brothers' floor-hugging sculptures. Lacking almost entirely the dimension of height, the sculptures dispel anthropomorphic associations. Yet a work such as Royden Rabinowitch's *Untitled 1975 No. 2* (fig. 56) actively engages the body of the viewer, who must move around it in order to construct a knowledge of its material and spatial properties from the experience of different views.

55. Ron Martin
(b. 1943)

Bright Red No. 8
1972
Acrylic on canvas
213 x 182 cm

56. Royden Rabinowitch
(b. 1943)

Untitled 1975 No. 2
1975
Cold-rolled steel,
blued and oiled
5.3 x 216.1 x 151.5 cm

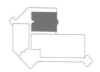
As artists continued their explorations of the boundaries between art and life, their range of materials and references also grew. Works incorporating industrially fabricated elements, images appropriated from the mass media, or found objects revealing their history through obvious signs of use have become more and more common.

In *Tarpaulin No. 3* (fig. 57; see also fig. 73) by Montreal artist Betty Goodwin, an old, discarded tarpaulin replaces the traditional canvas. Folded, draped, and thinly impregnated with gesso, the result is an evocative object that questions the limits of painting. Commonplace objects are also the source of Gathie Falk's ceramic sculptures, such as *Picnic with Birthday Cake and Blue Sky* (fig. 58), which transform the familiar with a touch of surrealist fantasy.

Out of an experimentation with materials and a desire to involve the spectator more directly, a new, hybrid form emerged called installation art. Made up of sculptural and pictorial elements placed in an environment that is thereby altered or even completely transformed, installations are diverse in theme. A changing selection of these works is on view in the second-level galleries, ranging from John Massey's highly personal evocation of dream imagery in *The Embodiment* (1976) to General Idea's museum-like assemblage of artifacts from a mythical beauty pavilion in *Reconstructing Futures* (1977).

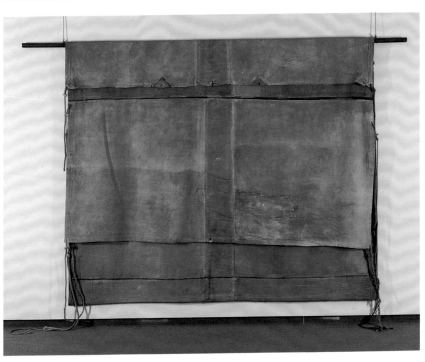

57. Betty Goodwin
(b. 1923)

Tarpaulin No. 3
1975
Gesso, pastel, chalk and
charcoal, with metal grommets
and rope on canvas
231 x 293.5 cm

58. Gathie Falk
(b. 1928)

*Picnic with Birthday Cake
and Blue Sky*
1976
Glazed ceramic, mounted in
painted wood and glass case
63.6 x 63.4 x 59.7 cm

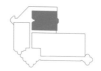

The contemporary world has been indelibly shaped by the advance of technology. Nowhere is this more obvious than in the mass media, where television, films, and advertising have surrounded us with images of an often distant and idealized reality. A concern with the forms and meanings of the everyday world has led many artists to adopt photographic media, to which they often bring a sophisticated awareness of earlier art as well as a critical view of the mass media's use of photography.

The work of Pierre Boogaerts or Jeff Wall reveals the growing importance of photography in contemporary art. Wall's *The Destroyed Room* (fig. 59) refers to the thinly disguised violence of commercial window displays at that time — evidence of the punk phenomenon's influence on our culture. A work about domestic aggression and revenge, *The Destroyed Room* also recalls Eugène Delacroix's painting *The Death of Sardanapalus* (1827), which linked eroticism and violence at the beginning of the modern, bourgeois era.

Despite the prevalence of three-dimensional and photographic work, painting has remained a vital form of expression. Certain painters, like Christopher Pratt of Newfoundland, worked in relative isolation from contemporary trends. His painting *The Visitor* (fig. 60) is done in a style of high realism that has little to do with the resurgence of figurative painting of the early 1980s.

Recent painting is more difficult to categorize, as it is not guided by any one theoretical perspective. Its very openness has made it an attractive vehicle for a wide range of ideas and styles, from the feminism of Mary Scott to the ongoing engagement with the precepts of modernism in recent paintings by Ron Martin and Guido Molinari.

59. Jeff Wall
(b. 1946)

The Destroyed Room
1978
Cibachrome transparency,
fluorescent light, display case
159 x 229 cm

60. Christopher Pratt
(b. 1935)

The Visitor
1977
Oil on masonite
95.6 x 226.8 cm

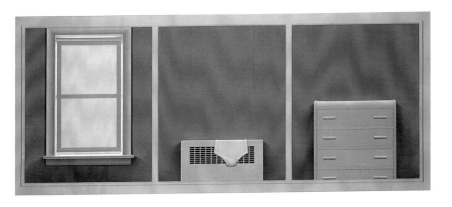

During the post-war period in which the United States emerged as a
world power, the centre of the art world also shifted from Paris to
New York. By the late fifties the subjective style and heroic rhetoric
associated with Abstract Expressionism was yielding to a newly objective
spirit, characterized by a desire to focus on the real world.

The work of Claes Oldenburg and George Segal forms a bridge between
Abstract Expressionism and Pop Art, so-called because it took its subject matter from popular consumer culture. Originally a painter, Segal
transformed the figurative images in his paintings into life-sized
plaster figures, placing them in a setting of thoughtfully chosen objects.
Works such as *The Gas Station* (1963) capture a banal moment with
stark realism.

Politically and economically the sixties were a period of expansion,
which was reflected artistically in a desire for big dimensions and
visual impact. Many of the Pop artists, such as James Rosenquist, who
had been a billboard painter, and Andy Warhol, originally an illustrator,
used the large-scale, often repeated images of advertising techniques
to give their works a cool anonymity. Fascinated by the glamorous
packaging of ordinary things, Warhol saw no need to invent new images,
but simply reproduced the labelling of a familiar product in *Brillo*
(fig. 61).

61. Andy Warhol
(1928-1987)

Brillo
1964
Plywood boxes with silkscreen
and acrylic
43.2 x 43.2 x 35.6 cm

A desire for objectivity in reaction to the inward-looking painting of
the Abstract Expressionists also motivated a number of sculptors who
were working with geometric forms. Rejecting the illusionistic structures of traditional sculpture, Carl Andre, Dan Flavin, Donald Judd,
and Richard Serra made specific objects of great simplicity that earned
them the Minimalist label.

Some of the most radical work came from Andre and Flavin. Using
readily available industrial materials such as fluorescent lights, bricks,
and metal plates, they made works that transformed the space of the
viewer. Andre's *Lever* (fig. 62) is a single line of firebricks that cuts
across the space of the gallery. Highly controversial when first exhibited,
the work exemplifies his concept of sculpture as place.

62. Carl Andre
(b. 1935)

Lever
1966
137 firebricks
11.4 x 22.5 x 883.9 cm

Flavin's installations of fluorescent tubes create a luminous zone that
transforms the ambient space even more dramatically. Unlike Andre
or Judd, he does not reject associative meanings in his work. The
arrangement of lights in *monument 4 for those who have been killed
in ambush (to P.K. who reminded me about death)* (fig. 63) resembles
a gun emplacement, while the colour red reinforces the word "death"
of the title.

The era was marked by a continuing questioning of the limits of art.
The "dematerialization" of the work brought about by the artists
associated with Conceptual art was never complete, but the movement
did serve to shift attention from the object to the idea and the processes behind it. These works range from the purely verbal definition
of Joseph Kosuth's *Titled (Art as Idea as Idea)* (fig. 64) to German
artist Hans Haacke's *Condensation Cube* (1963-65), a closed system
that illustrates his interest in revealing the invisible processes of
the environment.

After a long period of American predominance, European painters
and sculptors once again gained widespread public attention. From
the German and Italian neo-expressionist painters (so-called because
of their gestural, figurative style), the collection includes a work by
Jörg Immendorff, entitled *Parade* (1984). Blending personal and
traditional symbolism, Immendorff's painting deals with the post-war
split of the two Germanies and the tensions that abound there.

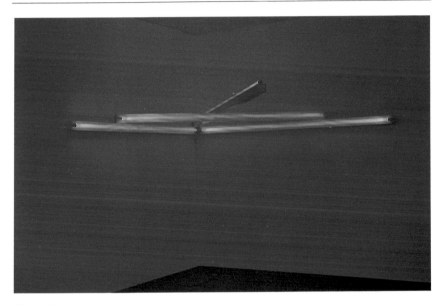

63. Dan Flavin
(b. 1933)

*monument 4 those who have
been killed in ambush (to P.K.
who reminded me about death)*
1966-69
Red fluorescent light
166.4 x 345.4 cm

64. Joseph Kosuth
(b. 1938)

Titled (Art as Idea as Idea)
1966-73
Photostat blow-up of
photograph
122 x 122 cm

box (1) (bɔks), *n.* Boîte, caisse, *f.*; comparti-
ment, cabinet particulier (at a restaurant etc.),
m.; malle; (*Theat.*) loge, *f.*; siège (on a
carriage); corps (of a pump); moyeu (of a
wheel), *m.*; maisonnette, *f.*, pied-à-terre
(country-house); (*Print.*) cassetin; buis (tree),
m. Christmas-box, *étrennes*, *f.pl.*; hunting-
box, *pavillon de chasse*, *m.*; sentry-box,
guérite, *f.*; snuff-box, *tabatière*, *f.*; strong-
box, *coffre-fort*, *m.*; to be in the wrong box,
se tromper, se fourvoyer. *v.t.* Enfermer dans
une boîte, encaisser. To box the compass,
savoir la rose des vents; revenir à son point
de départ.

The collection has focused particularly on the work of those innovative
British and European sculptors whose work flows from the conceptual
currents of the seventies. These sculptors have tended to draw their
inspiration from nature or from the castoffs of urban society, which
they incorporate into their work.

Nature remains the primary source for the work of British artist
Richard Long. His sculptures of stones or sticks arranged either in the
landscape or in the gallery into archetypal, formal structures of straight
lines, circles, and spirals all come from his walks across the land. He
views the walks themselves as artworks that define the form of the
land in space and time.

Like Long, Italian Giuseppe Penone's sculpture is derived from a close
affinity with nature. The idea of making the natural process of transformation visible is central to all his work. The early *8-Meter Tree*
(fig. 65) reverses the normal process of change, working back from the
beam to a sapling tree. In leaving one side of the beam untouched, he
reaffirms his act of cultural appropriation.

English artists Bill Woodrow and Tony Cragg look to the stuff of urban
life, the throw-away world of mass-produced, consumable objects.
Whereas Cragg's assemblages are a kind of drawing with objects,
Woodrow treats junk as a primary material from which he makes new
things. Much of the humour of these objects comes from their impro-
visational air; however, the humour in such environments as *Life on
Earth* (1984) has a black undercurrent that turns the attention back
to the chaotic reality of contemporary life.

65. Giuseppe Penone
(b. 1947)

8-Meter Tree
1969
Wood
10 x 19 x 800 cm

The National Gallery is unusual in that all of its video programming comes from tapes in its collection. It is one of the few North American museums to collect videotapes extensively, in recognition of the important place the work of video artists enjoys in contemporary art. The collection is composed entirely of independent, non-commercial productions made outside the mainstream of the television industry and represents a diverse selection of genres and styles.

A relatively young art form, video dates its beginnings from the availability of portable, "home" video equipment that provided artists with an accessible yet challenging new medium. Sometimes referred to as "television by artists," video has flickered in the shadow of its technological parent, television. Today video remains rooted in the social context from which it grew, namely, community groups and artist-run centres.

The collection is made up predominantly of Canadian work, but it also includes tapes by artists from Japan, Great Britain, France, the United States, Chile, and Brazil. Among the Canadian artists represented are Lisa Steele, Julien Poulin and Pierre Falardeau, Colin Campbell, General Idea, Paul Wong, Co-op Vidéo de Montréal, and Norman Cohn.

Videotapes are shown in a specially-designed gallery space on the second level of the contemporary wing. Here, in a comfortable viewing/reading room, the visitor may consult a wide range of information on video and on its production and distribution network in Canada, including programme notes and catalogues on video works.

The Gallery has assembled a small collection of experimental films by artists whose work is represented elsewhere in the collection. Highlights include films by Michael Snow, Joyce Wieland, Charles Gagnon, Jack Chambers, and American artist Nancy Graves.

In addition, regular programmes of documentaries, dramatic works, and experimental films are screened in the Gallery's 400-seat theatre, which is equipped with both 16 and 35 mm projection facilities.

The Gallery is justifiably proud of its Canadian prints and drawings collection. With over 6,000 works, it is significant not only for its size, but also for its unique character: it is the only comprehensive collection of Canadian watercolours, prints, and drawings spanning the period from the mid-eighteenth century to the present.

Although the collection attempts to represent the best in prints and
drawings from all regions of Canada and all periods of artistic activity,
its strength lies in its holdings of the works of major artists. Highlights
of the collection include a portfolio of academic drawings by François
Baillairgé (1759-1830) made between 1778 and 1781, a remarkable
group of watercolours (see fig. 67) by the military artist Thomas
Davies, as well as large bodies of work by Ozias Leduc (1864-1955),
L.L. FitzGerald (see fig. 68), David Milne (1882-1953), A.Y. Jackson
(1882-1974), Walter J. Phillips (see fig. 70), Clarence Gagnon (1881-
1942), Edwin Holgate (1892-1977), Carl Schaefer (b. 1903), Charles
Henry White (1878-1918), and H. Ivan Neilson (1865-1931).

Other features include a superb collection of watercolours, with examples from every period, woodblock prints from the 1920s and 1930s,
and abstract expressionist prints from the 1950s and early 1960s by
artists such as Albert Dumouchel (see fig. 71) and Yves Gaucher, which
established Canada's reputation internationally as one of the leaders
in fine art prints.

66. François Beaucourt
(1740-1794)

Portrait of a Young Girl
1787
Coloured chalks and charcoal
on laid paper
34.8 x 27.8 cm

67. Thomas Davies
(c. 1737-1812)

Montreal
1812
Watercolour over graphite on
wove paper
34.2 x 52.2 cm

68. L.L. FitzGerald
(1890-1956)

Abstract Landscape
1942
Coloured chalk on wove paper
61 x 46 cm
Gift from the
Douglas M. Duncan
Collection, 1970

The collection originated at the end of the last century and consisted
of a few watercolours from the artists of the Royal Canadian Academy, in
particular Lucius R. O'Brien (1832-1899) and Daniel Fowler (1810-1894).
It was not until 1910, on the initiative of Sir Edmund Walker, a
member of the Arts Advisory Committee, that a meaningful effort
was made to build a prints and drawings collection. At that time the
Gallery acquired its first prints, including Elizabeth Armstrong Forbes's
exquisite *Dorothy (No. 2)* (fig. 72).

Until 1954, acquisitions consisted of (with the odd exception) contemporary works. In that year, the purchase of twenty watercolours
by Thomas Davies, ranging from 1757 to 1812, established a strong
foundation for a historical collection. In 1970, a major portion of
Douglas M. Duncan's collection of prints and drawings was donated
to the Gallery, including nearly 300 works by L.L. FitzGerald and
the important Milne–Duncan Bequest of approximately 150 colour
drypoints by David Milne. That same year the Gallery purchased a
significant part of the W.H. Coverdale Collection of Canadiana from
the Manoir Richelieu, which included watercolours by important British garrison artists such as James Pattison Cockburn (1779-1847),
Charles R. Forrest (c. 1787-1827), and George Heriot (1759-1839).

69. Paul Kane
(1810-1871)

*The Death of Omoxesisixany
or Big Snake*
c. 1856
Embossed colour woodblock
on wove paper
(sheet and image)
37 x 46.2 cm

70. Walter J. Phillips
(1884-1963)

Karlukwees, B.C.
1929
Colour woodcut on japan paper
26.6 x 31.8 cm (block)

In 1973, Gallery Director Jean Sutherland Boggs decided to develop the
Canadian prints and drawings collection and placed it under the responsibility of its own curator. Since that time the collection has expanded
significantly through a consistent and well-defined acquisitions policy,
which includes both contemporary and historical Canadian works.

Because of their fragility, the prints and drawings are exhibited in
rotation for limited periods in the Prints, Drawings, and Photographs
galleries on the second level. Specific works may be viewed by
appointment in the Prints, Drawings, and Photographs study room
in the curatorial wing.

71. Albert Dumouchel
(1916-1971)

The Mantle of Cold
1963
Colour etching on wove paper
45.5 x 60.5 cm (plate)

72. Elizabeth Armstrong Forbes
(1859-1912)

Dorothy (No. 2)
1881-83
Drypoint in brown on laid paper
19.8 x 12.3 cm (plate)
Gift of Stanhope A. Forbes and
2d Lt. W.A.S. Forbes, 1916

73. Betty Goodwin
(b. 1923)

Vest with Plaster and Feathers
1974
Collage
61 x 45.7 cm

European and American
Prints and Drawings

The European and American prints and drawings collection, which comprises more than 1,200 drawings and 6,500 prints, is the most extensive in Canada and among the finest in North America. Notable both for its excellence and diversity, the collection represents all the major schools from the fifteenth century to the present day.

The National Gallery collects prints above all for their artistic merit, but it also endeavours to assemble a representative selection of a particular printmaker's work. It is only through an analysis of a significant part of an artist's production that we are able to follow his personal and stylistic evolution and to appreciate the full range of his graphic expression. For example, the Gallery now owns over one hundred works by M.C. Escher, which were recently donated by his son, George A. Escher (see fig. 74). The Gallery has also acquired a large number of nineteenth-century French prints with the specific intention of illustrating the development of such print techniques as lithography.

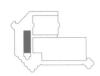
For its somewhat smaller drawing collection, the Gallery is fortunate
to acquire from time to time the preparatory sketches for works of art
already in its possession. Among the most remarkable is a pen-and-
ink drawing entitled *Nude Woman with a Staff* (fig. 75) by Albrecht
Dürer, which was a preliminary study for the figure of Eve in the
engraving *The Fall of Man* (1504). Also part of the collection is a
final study (discovered in 1984 and acquired by means of a Canadian
government grant) for the celebrated painting *The Death of General
Wolfe* by Benjamin West (see fig. 36). This famous historical subject
inspired the drawing by Louis-Joseph Watteau (1731-1798) entitled
The Death of Montcalm (c. 1783), which forms a fascinating pendant
to Wolfe's work.

In addition to these well-known works are a number of large sets or
suites of prints, as well as important individual drawings. One of
the highlights from the Italian School is the complete set of *Carceri*
(Prisons) in both states by Giovanni Battista Piranesi (1720-1778). By
comparing the first state (c. 1745) to the second (c. 1760), one can see
the evolution of the etchings in the added detail and in the dramatic
reworking of light and shade. Another outstanding work is the important Italian Renaissance print by Antonio Pollaiuolo, *Battle of Naked
Men* (fig. 76). A delightful drawing by Giovanni Domenico Tiepolo
(1727-1804), *An Encounter during a Country Walk* (c. 1791), which
was a gift of Mrs. Samuel Bronfman in honour of her husband,
represents the wit and charm of the eighteenth century.

74. M.C. Escher
(1898-1972)

Möbius Strip II
1963
Wood engraving in red, black,
and green on laid paper
53.2 x 23.8 cm
Gift of George A. Escher, 1984

The Spanish collection is notable for its print series by Francisco
Goya (1746-1828), including the complete *Caprichos* (1797-99), the
Disasters of War (1810-20), and the *Tauromaquia* (1815-16). Another
highlight is the *Vollard Suite* (1930-37) by Pablo Picasso (1881-1973),
one hundred prints of classical and mythological subjects featuring
the sculptor, his model, and the minotaur, where the artist illustrates
a favourite theme, the human body, in particular the female body.
Picasso's deeply moving *Weeping Woman* (1937) reveals yet another,
expressionistic aspect of his printmaking.

Among the most important prints from the Flemish School is the
Iconography (c. 1625-41) by Anthony van Dyck (1599-1641), a series
of 292 portraits, some of them etched by the artist himself, representing
contemporary humanists as well as artistic and political celebrities.
From the Dutch School, some thirty works by Rembrandt (1606-1669)
reveal this great master of graphic art at his finest, including the pen-
and-ink drawing *The Baptism of the Ethiopian Eunuch* (c. 1652-55),
the well-known print *The Three Trees* (1643), and the etched portrait
Jan Lutma, Goldsmith (1656).

75. Albrecht Dürer
(1471-1528)

Nude Woman with a Staff
c. 1501-03
Pen and brown ink and
brown wash on paper
23.5 x 9.6 cm
Gift of Joseph Hirshhorn and
a group of friends, 1956

76. Antonio Pollaiuolo
(1432-1498)

Battle of Naked Men
c. 1470
Engraving on laid paper
41.8 x 61.1 cm

The collection is particularly strong in eighteenth- and nineteenth-century English drawings and in French nineteenth-century prints. Memorable selections from these schools include *Oak Tree, Shoreham, Kent* (fig. 77) by English watercolourist Samuel Palmer and the *Large Bathers* (fig. 78), a lithograph with watercolour by Paul Cézanne. *Dancer Resting in an Armchair* (fig. 79) by Henri Matisse is a superb example of a twentieth-century drawing by a modern European master.

The modern Russian School has taken on a new importance in the collection with the recent acquisition of the suite of colour lithographs *Daphnis et Chloé* (fig. 80) by Marc Chagall, a gift of Félix Quinet in memory of Joseph and Marguerite Liverant.

The United States is represented principally by artists who have been at the heart of the major movements of modern art, among them Pop artists Jim Dine (b. 1935) with his portfolio of collages and silkscreens *A Tool Box* (1966), and Andy Warhol (1928-1987) with his

77. Samuel Palmer
(1805-1881)

Oak Tree, Shoreham, Kent
c. 1828
Pen and brown ink, and
graphite, with watercolour,
gouache, and opaque white,
heightened with gum arabic
on grey wove paper
29.5 x 46.8 cm

78. Paul Cézanne
(1839-1906)

Large Bathers
1896-c. 1898
Lithograph with watercolour
on laid paper
48.8 x 63.8 cm

silkscreen series *Flash - November 22, 1963* (1968) and *Mao Tse-tung* (1972). The Gallery also owns *Study for "Woman I"* (fig. 81) by Willem de Kooning, a drawing of considerable importance in the history of Abstract Expressionism.

The fine reputation that the collection enjoys today is due in large measure to Kathleen Fenwick, its first curator. Throughout a long career at the Gallery, she encouraged the development of the prints and drawings department and by her judicious and discriminating acquisitions endowed it with a core of master works. Succeeding curators have successfully built on and expanded her legacy.

Because of their fragility, prints and drawings are exhibited in rotation and for limited periods in a gallery on the second level, next to Inuit Art. Specific works from the collection may be viewed by appointment in the Prints, Drawings, and Photographs study room in the curatorial wing.

79. Henri Matisse
(1869-1954)

Dancer Resting in an Armchair
1939
Charcoal on wove paper
63.9 x 47.8 cm

80. Marc Chagall
(1887-1985)

Noon in Summer from
Daphnis et Chloé
1957-61
Colour lithograph on
wove paper
41.1 x 31.8 cm
Gift of Félix Quinet, 1986

81. Willem de Kooning
(b. 1904)

Study for "Woman I"
c. 1952
Graphite and pastel on
wove paper
31 x 29 cm

The collection of contemporary Inuit art acquired by the National Gallery attests to the vitality of the fine arts in the Arctic and in particular to the imagination and talent of its artists.

Established in 1960 by Kathleen Fenwick, curator of prints and drawings, the collection then consisted of approximately thirty prints. Among the first works to be made at the Cape Dorset printshop, they were acquired for their undeniable aesthetic quality and originality. The prints include Tudlik's (1890-1966) *Division of Meat* (1959), Parr's *Men and Walrus* (fig. 82), and Kenojuak's (b. 1927) *The Enchanted Owl* (1960), perhaps the most famous Inuit print, in which the artist presents one of her favourite subjects in a peacock-like pose.

Because of important donations (including those from M.F. Feheley and Dr. Dorothy M. Stillwell) and purchases since 1984, the collection has grown substantially and is now under the responsibility of a curator. Although its aim is to represent the prints, drawings, and sculpture produced since 1949, the year that marks the beginnings of contemporary Inuit art, the focus of the collection is primarily on the outstanding individual artists and on the major works by other artists from across the Canadian Arctic.

Significant examples of prints and drawings by Pitseolak (c. 1904-1983), Pudlo, and Jessie Oonark are being added to the collection in order to demonstrate the talents of these artists. Pitseolak's scenes of everyday life, oral traditions, and mythology, rendered in fluid, dynamic lines and warm colours, reveal her characteristic verve and humour. Sensitive to the reality of living in the Arctic in the computer age, Pudlo presents a universe of paradox where traditional Inuit culture rubs shoulders with modern technology. *Large Loon and Landscape* (fig. 83) attests to the uniqueness of this artist's vision and his masterly draughtsmanship. Jessie Oonark applied to her graphic work the same principles she used in her tapestries. In *Woman* (fig. 84), the artist elaborates a favoured theme of depicting an Inuit woman dressed in the parka of the central Arctic; in constructing the image she abstracts the elements of the costume, juxtaposing geometric forms with contrasting colours.

Until recently, Inuit artists have been known mainly for their prints; their drawings, however, reveal another dimension of their art. Although sometimes used as the basis for prints, the drawings are usually conceived as complete and independent works. Some of the most interesting drawings come from artist-hunters such as Parr and Kiakshuk (1888-1966), who firmly ensconced in the traditional ways, draw their world with a vitality and directness that springs from an intuitive sense of technique and composition.

Other highlights of the prints and drawings collection are Kenojuak's stone-cut print *The Owl* (1969), along with its drawing and stone, as well as her drawing for *The Enchanted Owl* (1960).

Inuit sculptors, working with material at hand such as soapstone, bone, and ivory, are inspired by their natural environment, the people, and their own mythology. *Man and Bear* (fig. 85), attributed to Palosee,

82. Parr
(1893-1969)

Men and Walrus
1961
Stonecut on wove japan paper
54.4 x 29 cm (image)

83. Pudlo
(b. 1916)

Large Loon and Landscape
1981
Colour lithograph on
wove paper
56.7 x 76.5 cm
(sheet and image)
Gift of
Dorothy M. Stillwell, M.D.,
1985

84. Jessie Oonark
(1906-1985)

Woman
1970
Colour stonecut and stencil on
wove paper
62.2 x 40.2 cm (image)
Gift of
Dorothy M. Stillwell, M.D.,
1985

and carved from a small vertebrae, is an excellent example of the sculptor's ingenuity in exploiting the properties and small scale of indigenous material.

Among the strengths of the sculpture collection are the many fine works by Osuitok, one of Canada's most accomplished and consistently original sculptors. His *Walrus Spirit* (fig. 86) depicts a woman's body with the enormous, deformed head of a walrus. Reflecting the coming together of man and animal life, possibly related to the shaman's power of transformation, it is a familiar theme in Inuit art.

Another masterpiece is Abraham Angnakak's (b. 1937) *Memory of an Old Game* (1969-74), which represents the embrace of a man and a woman. Carved out of whale bone, the sculpture manifests not only the artist's vision, but also his skill in manipulating such porous material and in using its various tonalities to his advantage.

Inuit Art is located on the second level, next to Prints, Drawings, and Photographs. Access is through a small octagonal room reserved primarily for sculpture. An adjoining room is devoted to prints and drawings, which are exhibited in rotation for limited periods. Specific works from the collection can be viewed by appointment in the Prints, Drawings, and Photographs study room in the curatorial wing.

85. Attributed to Palosee

Man and Bear
c. 1971
Bone (vertebrae)
6.4 x 4.6 x 4.5 cm
Gift of
Dorothy M. Stillwell, M.D.,
1985

86. Osuitok
(b. 1922)

Walrus Spirit
c. 1977
Dark-green stone and ivory
46 x 20 x 32.5 cm
Gift of M.F. Feheley, 1985

Photographs

The National Gallery has been involved with photography through its exhibition programmes since 1934, but it was not until the spring of 1967 that the Gallery began to collect photographs. A broad collecting policy soon took shape, which included rare, vintage prints of the early years of the medium as well as work by living photographers. Its purpose was to illustrate the history of photography as an image-making process rather than as a technical concern.

Among the first purchases was a large group of works by Charles Nègre (see fig. 87), now numbering 185, which has become one of the collection's major attractions. This purchase was followed by the acquisition of the work of William Henry Fox Talbot (1800-1877), inventor of the negative-positive process. These 145 prints and negatives, which include work pre-dating 1839, the official birth-year of photography, as well as the later, mature photographs, provide insights into the evolution of his invention. A collection of 175 works by David Octavius Hill (1802-1870), the first trained painter to put Talbot's process to a serious artistic use (along with his partner, Robert Adamson) completed the historical basis for the collection.

At present the collection numbers over 16,000 images. Not all have been produced by well-known photographers; some would not have even considered themselves seriously as artists. But all the works have been chosen for their ability to heighten perception, stimulate the mind, delight the eye, arouse emotion, or contribute to our understanding of the nature of the medium.

A museum collection, by its very nature, serves a varied public. Both the general viewer searching for personal enjoyment and the scholar requiring extensive resources for serious research must be satisfied. Therefore, in addition to breadth, emphasis has been placed on collecting in depth. More so than paintings, photographs tend to function sequentially. Where one or two photographs will tell us little of the photographer's vocabulary and concerns, many will open the door to understanding.

The strengths of the collection lie in nineteenth-century English, French, German, American, and Middle-Eastern topographical images and portraiture, as well as in the beginnings of the pictorial movement with Julia Margaret Cameron (see fig. 88) and P.H. Emerson (1856-1936), which culminated in the work of the photo-secessionists in the early twentieth century. The beginnings of documentary photography can be traced from David Octavius Hill, the Crimean War, the Anglo-French expedition into China in 1860, and the American Civil War (represented by an important group of 500 images), to the work of Lewis Hine (1874-1940) in the early part of the century, and finally, to the images of the Photo League and of Walker Evans (see fig. 89) in the 1930s and 1940s.

87. Charles Nègre
(1820-1880)

Chimney-Sweeps Walking
1851
Salted paper print
15.2 x 19.8 cm

88. Julia Margaret Cameron
(1815-1879)

Alethia (Alice Liddell)
1872
Albumen silver print,
mounted on card
32.4 x 23.7 cm

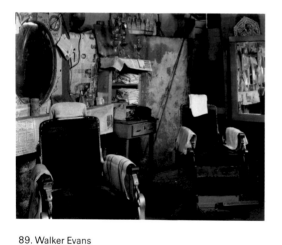

89. Walker Evans
(1903-1975)

*Negro Barber Shop,
Atlanta, Georgia*
1936
Gelatin silver print
19.1 x 23.8 cm
Gift of Phyllis Lambert, 1982

The exploration of the formal and expressive potential of photography can be seen not only in the work of Evans, but also in major collections by Eugène Atget (see fig. 90), Edward Weston (see fig. 91), Margaret Watkins, Josef Sudek (see fig. 92), Harry Callahan, Aaron Siskind, Minor White, Robert Frank, David Heath (see fig. 93), Diane Arbus, Eikoh Hosoe, and Nathan Lyons. The collection also includes the work of the younger photographers of the 1970s and 1980s such as Roger Mertin, Les Krims, Betty Hahn, Robert Fichter, Michael Bishop (see fig. 94), Lynn Cohen, Charles Gagnon, Tom Gibson, Stephen Livick, and Michael Schreier, to name only a few.

The range extends from the unassuming to the artful. At one extreme are the topographical photographers with no pretense to art, but who in their sensitivity produced work that transcends the original intention and that we find stimulating, significant, or moving today. At the other extreme are those men and women who thought of themselves as artists and the photographs they produced as works of art.

Photography is the visual memory of mankind, a storehouse of information and often a witness to things that no human being has ever seen or ever will see directly. Photographs can also reveal ourselves to ourselves in unsettling ways. The photograph becomes a model for a point in time that has been selected, purified, and offered for contemplation.

90. Eugène Atget
(1857-1927)

Saint-Cloud
1915-19
Albumen silver print
18.3 x 21.8 cm

91. Edward Weston
(1886-1958)

Toadstool
1931
Gelatin silver print, mounted
on buff-faced pasteboard
19.2 x 24 cm
Purchased from the
Phyllis Lambert Fund, 1979

92. Josef Sudek
(1896-1976)

Portrait of My Friend Funke
1924
Gelatin silver print
28.5 x 22.6 cm

Photographs are not enough in themselves, however, to explore the history and nature of the medium. The collection is supplemented by etchings, engravings, lithographs, and drawings relevant to the prehistory and early history of photography from the sixteenth century to 1925. A library of nineteenth- and twentieth-century photographic literature of both books and periodicals is available for research, including a complete run of *Camera Work* (1904-16) and *Galerie contemporaine* (1876-84).

Without the support and generosity of private citizens, the National Gallery's collection of photographs would not have achieved its present richness and variety. The nation owes a debt of gratitude to the donors of these gifts, especially to Phyllis Lambert, who has provided generous support for the collection both with financial gifts and by donations of major groups of work by early European daguerreotypists, American Civil War photographers, and Walker Evans, among others.

Because of their fragility, photographs are exhibited in rotation for limited periods in a gallery on the second level, next to Prints and Drawings. Works not on exhibition may be examined by appointment in the Prints, Drawings, and Photographs study room in the curatorial wing.

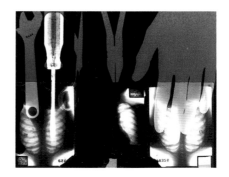

93. David Heath
(b. 1931)

Chicago
1956-62
Gelatin silver print
18.2 x 22.6 cm (image)

94. Michael Bishop
(b. 1946)

Untitled
1973
Gelatin silver print
22.8 x 30.5 cm (image)